DIM SUM AND OTHER
CHINESE STREET FOOD

Books by Mai Leung

The Classic Chinese Cookbook
The Chinese People's Cookbook

DIM SUM AND OTHER CHINESE STREET FOOD

MAI LEUNG

Drawings by Claude Martinot

HARDCOVER TITLE: *The Chinese People's Cookbook*

HARPER COLOPHON BOOKS
HARPER & ROW, PUBLISHERS
NEW YORK, CAMBRIDGE, PHILADELPHIA, SAN FRANCISCO
LONDON, MEXICO CITY, SÃO PAULO, SYDNEY

A hardcover edition of this book is published by Harper & Row, Publishers under the title *The Chinese People's Cookbook*.

DIM SUM AND OTHER CHINESE STREET FOOD. Copyright © 1979 by Yuk Mai Leung Thayer. All rights reserved. Printed in the United States of America. No part of this book may be used or reproduced in any manner whatsoever without written permission except in the case of brief quotations embodied in critical articles and reviews. For information address Harper & Row, Publishers, Inc., 10 East 53rd Street, New York, N.Y. 10022. Published simultaneously in Canada by Fitzhenry & Whiteside Limited, Toronto.

Designed by Janice Stern

First HARPER COLOPHON edition published 1982.

ISBN: 0-06-090919-6   (previously ISBN: 0-06-012598-5)

82 83 84 85 86 10 9 8 7 6 5 4 3 2 1

To Mother and Grandmother

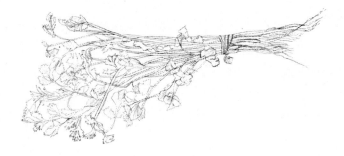

CONTENTS

ACKNOWLEDGMENTS

Several persons helped the development of this book at various points, and I am delighted to be able publicly to express my gratitude to them.

Frances McCullough, my editor, knew what I wanted to do and gave me leeway to do it. Besides being an excellent editor, her good nature and motherly encouragement gave life and strength to the book. Millie Owen, hawk-eyed in Vermont, is a meticulous, caring copy editor whom I could totally rely on. After Millie's red pencil cross-examined me a thousand times, Dolores Simon sifted through the manuscript with the patience and devotion of an old-time gold miner on some western hill. With unerring cheerfulness and enthusiasm she made final adjustments and guided it through production.

Gloria Adelson is responsible for the beautiful cover design. Janice Stern took charge of the layout of each page with gentle care, as she did for my first book. Claude Martinot again has provided the distinguished drawings which illustrate the text. Kathleen Hyde, calm and attentive as always, labored for my first book and continued her enthusiasm even while I worked on this one.

My friends Blair MacInness, Dee Shoaf, Peggy McDonnell, and Joan Leclerc provided support, made thoughtful suggestions, chopped, cooked, typed, and tasted. To them I offer warmest thanks.

But my special gratitude is reserved for my husband Nel: for without him at my side, no banquets or books could I have produced.

INTRODUCTION

Americans' appreciation and understanding of authentic Chinese food have burgeoned since China and the United States have resumed a more normal trading relationship. Innumerable cooking ingredients from China long absent from the States are now stacked high in Chinese grocery stores. And returning from Hong Kong, our suitcases are no longer laden with spices and herbs and "unidentified suspicious powders." (Once the U.S. customs officers sniffed for two hours, as if I were the Godmother of the Chinese Connection becoming careless.)

The abundance and availability of exotic ingredients have inspired some quality Chinese cookbooks, replacing those that were full of hopeless substitutions and half-learned information. Chop suey, egg rolls, and other so-called Chinese dishes are now acknowledged as a laughable aberration of the past. The fine regional food of Peking, Canton, Szechwan, Hunan, and Shanghai is offered in restaurants and taught in cooking classes. Recent cookbooks have advanced American palates into another dimension of Chinese gastronomy.

However, this fine Chinese food represents only half of the rich and manifold Chinese cuisine. What people in the United States commonly learn, enjoy, and think of as everyday Chinese fare is actually substantial dinner and banquet food for formal entertaining. The other half of the Chinese culinary tradition, the colorful daily fare of the Chinese, has not been discovered by most Westerners.

This book will focus on the exuberant and abundant breakfast, lunch, and snacks of China when she is most at ease and without formality. It invites you to partake of the exquisite dim sum breakfasts and luscious noodle and rice lunches of the teahouses. It acquaints you with the varieties of street food sold in sidewalk stalls by ambient vendors proud of their particular secrets, the festival food young and old cherish, the finger food to enjoy in theaters, the countless snacks to gladden a late evening of friendship, and the feast of the "poor people's nightclub" in which thousands of poor—and rich—idle under a skyful of stars.

Work on this book has taken years of hunting. Some recipes are the result of many seasons of roaming the streets and idling in teahouses and restaurants in China, Kowloon, and Hong Kong. Some were taught privately by chefs for a high price, but some cost only a few cartons of cigarettes. Some were given by my family and relatives. Some I put together myself. And some I caught with my furtive eyes while chatting with nuns as they were cooking for the temples in Macau and Lantau Island near Hong Kong. Wanting to learn more about tea, I went to Taiwan, putting my nose in its teas and its tea shrubs on stretches of hills, and prowling through all the old books on tea in the Chinese University of Hong Kong.

Needless to say, I hang out in New York's Chinatown frequently, scouting for new tastes, having my ten thousand and one dim sum breakfasts, lunches, and snacks, listening to conversations beyond my table. I also follow ambulances, police sirens, and the crowds—girlhood habits I have not outgrown.

The recipes here are selected from the bountiful variety within various regions of China. I have made a conscientious effort to include both those that I find the best and those that are most favored in China's daily life. I have also included many that are rare in this country. In order to maintain the authentic character, texture, and flavor, I have kept wherever possible to the traditional cooking methods and the original ingredients.

I have worked with the recipes many times, both abroad and at home. The recipes that deal with doughs have been tested in the cold winter, crisp fall, sultry summer, and humid spring, because the nature of doughs is shifty and temperamental as the weather.

Besides recipes, I have also put something more in these pages, for food and people are inseparable. The essence of food is flavor and aroma, but its spirit is the people who create it, enjoy it, and surround it. So you might take flight with me to my native land, to the people of China and Hong Kong, not in a tourist car looking through glass but among them. You will be with them in teahouses munching crisp crescents, sipping tea, and sharing noodles in kitchens, at street stalls, in private homes when they are unrestricted by company manners, their spirits buoyant, bantering, alive, and bursting with energy.

I hope this book will provide those looking for new Chinese dishes with novel flavor and new delight.

Mai Leung

Madison, New Jersey
Moon Festival, 1978

BEFORE BEGINNING

1. Read the entire recipe carefully before preparing the ingredients.

2. Have all the ingredients ready and organized as directed in the Preparation of Ingredients.

• A dagger (†) means that portion of the recipe can be prepared several hours in advance.

• Ingredients such as meat, poultry, and seafood can be cut in advance. It is easier to cut meat and poultry if they are half-frozen (put them in the freezer for about 30 minutes). After they are cut, be sure to keep them covered and refrigerated until use. Use a food processor only when specified, and never for chopping onions, or they will turn bitter.

• Always cover the sauce mixture if it is prepared in advance. The vegetables, ginger, garlic, and scallions can be cut hours ahead. Put them in plastic bags, in covered jars, or on plates covered with plastic or foil wrap.

3. All measurements should be exactly as in the recipe.

• If the measure is by spoon, especially the sauce mixture, it should always be a level spoon. Level it with a knife.

• Do not add more than the recipe calls for; adding a few more ounces of vegetable, meat, poultry, or seafood to a stir-fried dish will make the dish bland and cause it to lose its special taste. (If you need more than the recipe calls for, repeat the recipe.) To ensure making no mistake, weigh ingredients. Exact measurement is essential for the success of these recipes. A scale is an indispensable aid to satisfactory results.

4. Batter and dough are temperamental, easily changed by the weather. So always pour in the water gradually when you prepare them. In humid weather you might need less water than in dry and crisp weather. No teacher can give exact instructions covering all conditions, so use your own judgment as needed.

5. Using the right kinds of soy sauce is essential for the authenticity and taste of the dishes. Do not substitute with Japanese or domestic soy sauces.

6. This book is based on cooking on a gas stove. Since an electric range is not as adjustable as a gas one, you may need to adjust the heat as on page 184 (see Cooking on Electric Stoves).

DIM SUM

DIM SUM AND THE CHINESE TEAHOUSE

Dim sum are dainty delicacies, crescents or buns filled with meat or seafood, steamed in small bamboo baskets, and delicate salty or sweet fried pastries presented on small plates. The name "dim sum" means literally "delight your heart." All of the dim sum are served fresh, handmade by the dim sum chefs and helpers through the night, then steamed or fried by a second crew of chefs and helpers just before they are brought to the customers.

Served in the morning, dim sum are the main attraction of the Chinese teahouse, which is a cultural phenomenon in itself. There is always a teahouse wherever you go in the Orient. Some are big with red pillars and gleaming orange-yellow roofs; many have tables in a garden among scented flowers and lotus ponds; a few are huge houseboats carved to look like dragons floating on the water. But most of them are just plain, unornamented regular restaurants.

Regular patrons of a teahouse arrive early in the morning. These are the waiters' choice customers, many of them having come for years, never missing a day. Many of them are men, known by name to the waiters, who loyally reserve their places. Newspapers in hand, without further conversation these patrons exchange brief greetings and take their familiar seats. Their favorite tea, robust Pu-Erh or one of the mild, fragrant varieties, is brought without having to be ordered—a silent honor given only to these regular patrons. Then, leaning back, they continue their daily ritual by unfolding their newspapers and from within the printed sanctuary survey the world in tranquility.

Others chat leisurely over a cup of tea, one ear attending to conversation and one to the singsong of the waitresses, called dim sum maids. Strolling languorously behind their dim sum carts, in slow, singsong voices they call out the names of the particular dim sum on their carts: "Shao . . . Mai . . . Cha . . . Siu . . . Bau. . . ."

When hearts and tastes are satisfied, those who need to work reluctantly head for the door, leaving a generous tip to secure the warm welcome of tomorrow. Those who stay stretch and make themselves comfortable, some easing out of their shoes, and some perhaps chatting amiably across the tables.

At about eleven-thirty, while the floor is swept, the lunch menus are brought to the tables. The regulars know that unless they are staying for lunch, they must go.

The lunch crowd consists of drop-in customers of all ages and sexes. On weekends, families troop in about eleven o'clock, have tea and dim sum, then stay for lunch.

For lunch, the teahouses serve countless kinds of noodles and rice dishes topped with assorted meat and vegetables. Some noodles are pan-fried until partly crispy, some are served in tasty soups, and some are tossed with sauce and a mixture of delicious ingredients.

Rice dishes are also many: fried rice of different kinds; seasoned rice with assorted meats wrapped and steamed in lotus leaves; plain rice topped with pieces of luscious roasted duck or soy chicken; or tender vegetables with shredded meat, chicken, or seafood in gravy spread on rice.

In the afternoon from three to six, the teahouses are slow. It is too late for lunch and too early for supper. But few teahouses can afford to close for the day. Most turn into regular restaurants when night falls; some are even transformed into American-style nightclubs or cabarets.

At these late afternoon hours, the choice of food is limited. But those who drift in are not there primarily for food but for other reasons: some are tired and come to sit before going home; some come to share a grievance, to voice an injustice; some come to give opinions and offer sound advice; some come because coming is a tradition; some come for dinner, hours early, having no other place. But most come for the familiar faces and the conversation that one can participate in, listen to, or ignore as folly.

In the spirit of the teahouse, you too can serve steamed crescents in small bamboo steamer baskets and delicate fried flaky salty or sweet pastries for brunch or as appetizers. Or have a generous dish of rice or noodles for lunch, dinner, or a late evening snack. Accompany this with a pot of your favorite tea among friends and family, and the best teahouse is within your own walls.

CRISPY DIM SUM

(Finger Delicacies and Appetizers)

CHEFS' PUFF-CRISP BATTER

One of the most important skills required of a dim sum chef is to be able to prepare a good batter. Every one seems able to whisk up a batter, but few can make it stay crisp over a long period after it is fried.

This batter represents the combined wisdom of several chefs given to me years ago: "Throw in flour and some baking powder, add enough oil to hold the flour, then add water. Stay to the thick side."

After hours of playing with batter, I realized it was the best batter one ever could taste. This batter produces a crust that is extremely light and crisp. Also, foods coated with it can be cooked in advance and kept in a low oven (150 degrees) for about 30 to 45 minutes without losing crispness.

PREPARATION OF INGREDIENTS

1 cup all-purpose flour, unsifted
1 tablespoon baking powder
¼ teaspoon salt
5 tablespoons vegetable oil
⅔ cup cold water
⅓ cup minced scallions, including some green
1 tablespoon white sesame seeds (optional)

DIRECTIONS FOR COOKING

1. Combine flour, baking powder, and salt in a mixing bowl. Stir in oil, and mix until a ball is loosely formed. Stir in water gradually, and mix into a thick smooth batter. Add scallions and sesame seeds (if you like), and mix.

2. Before frying, test whether consistency of the batter is right. Dip food in batter, then hold it over the bowl. The batter should drip down very slowly from food. If it does not drip at all, the batter is too thick; add a few drops of water and mix well.

If batter quickly runs off from food, it is too thin. You might need to start the batter from the beginning.

Notes: Oil for deep-frying has to reach deep-fry temperature (375 degrees), and it must be deep enough for the food to float.

If the oil is not hot enough, the batter will flow away from the food or settle with the food at the bottom of the pan.

When the oil's temperature is right, the batter puffs up, staying with the food, and floats to the surface at once. Do not turn food until batter becomes firm.

The batter should turn brown gradually. If it turns brown right away, turn off heat or lower the temperature.

BASIC CHINESE FLAKY PASTRY

Makes about 26 circles

This pastry is extremely flaky, and so light that it melts in your mouth. It is also easy to make; no fuss and no repeated refrigeration, for this pastry does not go into the oven but is fried in hot oil.

INGREDIENTS

INNER DOUGH

4 tablespoons lard or shortening
1 cup all-purpose flour

OUTER DOUGH

1 ½ cups all-purpose flour
1 ½ teaspoons sugar
3 tablespoons lard or shortening
6 to 7 tablespoons cold water

DIRECTIONS FOR MIXING THE DOUGH

1. In a mixing bowl, place inner dough ingredients. Rub lard or shortening and flour together with fingers. Press and form mixture into a smooth firm dough. If it seems loose, add a little more lard to hold it together. Put aside.

2. In another mixing bowl, place outer dough ingredients. Mix with fingers, then knead until the dough is soft, not sticky but smooth. If it seems stiff, wet your hand with water and knead until soft. Roll dough into a round ball, then (with a rolling pin) roll it into a circle large enough to wrap the ball of inner dough.

3. Wrap inner dough with outer dough into a ball. Pinch and smooth the opening by slapping and rolling the dough in your palms to keep it round.

4. Put dough on a floured surface. With a floured rolling pin, roll out dough into a ⅛-inch-thick rectangular sheet, turning sheet from time to time. Fold narrow ends toward each other to

meet at the center. Fold sheet in half lengthwise. Roll dough as thin as possible into a large sheet. Use a round 3-inch cookie cutter or a water glass to press and cut dough into round circles. Cover with a damp cloth to keep from drying. The circles are ready to be filled according to the recipes. (You may prepare the circles in advance and refrigerate them until ready to be filled.)

SPRING ROLL SKINS

(CHINESE CREPES)

Makes about 60

These translucent crepes are the authentic Chinese spring roll skins which are often confusingly labeled as egg roll skins on packages sold in the States.

Making these thin crepes is not easy. It requires hard work, practice, fast hands, learning to feel the right consistency of the dough and the correct heat for the griddle. So do be patient if your hard work does not yield many crepes the first try. To succeed in making these crepes, give your hands more practice, more chances to feel for the right consistency.

However, you may purchase them in Chinese grocery stores if you do not wish to make your own. They are handmade daily by skilled hands in Chinatowns, then packed in plastic bags for sale. They keep well for months in your freezer if the package is tightly sealed (no need to separate each skin). But be sure you buy the handmade variety and not those made by machine.

The handmade ones are round, soft, less even, and less uniform in thinness. The machine-made ones are usually square, very smooth, even and thin: imported from the Orient, they are usually sold frozen and are unreliable, sometimes falling apart in hot oil. Also, there are skins available for making American egg rolls (for Americans only); they are actually noodle sheets cut into large squares, and are not as crisp and delicate as the handmade crepes or spring roll skins. Use them only if you have no possibility of making or obtaining the other authentic ones.

PREPARATION OF INGREDIENTS

2 cups cold water
1 teaspoon salt
4 cups all-purpose flour: sift

DIRECTIONS FOR COOKING

1. Mix water and salt in a large mixing bowl. Add flour 1 cup at a time, stir, mix, and knead by hand for about 30 minutes or until dough is absolutely homogenized and toffeelike. Transfer it to a

clean bowl. Cover bowl with a damp cloth and let dough rest at room temperature for 4 to 6 hours. It can be kept in refrigerator overnight, but bring it back to room temperature before use.

2. Half of the success of making these crepes depends on a suitable pan or griddle. It should be heavy and spread its heat evenly. It can be a large cast-iron frying pan, or heavy griddle, or a crepe pan. Sometimes it may even work better to turn a pan upside down and use its bottom to make the crepes.

3. Wash and dry griddle or pan, because it must be free of grease.

4. Heat griddle or pan over low heat. Grasp a large handful of dough from bowl with one hand. Turn dough up and work it in your hand to round it and to center it, because the dough tends to flow. Quickly press the lump of dough onto the center of the griddle or pan and pull dough back immediately. A thin layer of crepe, about 6 inches in diameter, will adhere to the pan. When the crepe's edges begin to dry, lift edges with fingers and peel gently and put it on a plate under a damp cloth.

5. Before making another crepe, wipe griddle or pan with a dry towel to remove any particle that is left there. Make the other crepes in the same manner.

6. Crepes do not stick to each other. Stack and seal them between foil. They keep well in refrigerator for a few days, and they can be frozen. Thaw in foil before use.

Notes: If the dough becomes dry, add a few drops of water and work with hands until the consistency is right again. If the dough is too wet, do not add flour! But swing dough about your hand to allow water to evaporate.

If dough fails to adhere to griddle or pan, lower the heat and wipe griddle or pan with a damp cloth so that it is not too hot.

If crepes dry and break, the dough is too wet and the griddle or pan is too hot. Work the dough by swirling it about your hand to evaporate some water, and wipe the griddle or pan with a damp cloth to lower the heat.

If crepes are lumpy and thick, the dough is not homogeneous and is too dry. Work dough with a little water until it is thoroughly homogeneous.

If the griddle or pan is not hot enough, the crepe will stick to the griddle. Heat griddle or pan longer before making another crepe.

SHAO-MAI SKINS (OR WONTON SKINS)

Makes 90 to 95 skins

These skins are made fresh daily in Chinatown. Most of them are excellent, very thin and uniform. They are also inexpensive: a package containing more than one hundred skins costs about sixty to eighty cents. The Chinese do not make them at home.

If you cannot obtain them in your area, or want to make your own, follow the recipe, adding some muscle and patience, and you will be rewarded.

The skins can be made days in advance. Also, they freeze well in stacks if wrapped and sealed tightly; thaw before use.

INGREDIENTS

4 eggs
¼ cup water
½ teaspoon salt
3 cups all-purpose flour
about ½ cup cornstarch for dusting

DIRECTIONS FOR MAKING DOUGH

BY HAND

1. Beat eggs, water, and salt together until eggs become slightly foamy.

2. Put flour in a large mixing bowl and make a well in the center. Add egg mixture gradually to the flour and mix with hands to form a rough dough. (If you have a food processor, you may add flour and egg mixture directly in the bowl and beat with the metal blade for a few seconds or until a smooth dough is formed.) If dough seems stiff, wet your hands with water and knead until dough becomes soft. Wash hands.

3. Turn dough onto a floured surface. Knead until dough becomes homogenized and elastic.

4. Put dough in a lightly floured plastic bag to rest at room

temperature for about 30 minutes.

5. Roll dough into a sausage, then divide it into 20 equal portions. Roll each portion into a round ball and cover with a towel to prevent drying out.

6. Take one ball at a time, and roll it on a floured surface with a rolling pin until it becomes a very thin skin, almost transparent. If the skin seems thick, pull and stretch skin at one end, downward with one hand, while the other hand presses the skin at the other end with the rolling pin. Dust skin generously with cornstarch. Cover with a towel. Prepare the other skins in the same manner.

7. For wonton skins, stack and cut skins into 3-inch-square pieces. For shao-mai skins, trim squares into circles. Cover the stack. They are ready to be used.

BY NOODLE MACHINE

1. Prepare dough as above, from step 1 through step 4.

2. Dust work surface with flour. Roll dough into a sausage and divide it into six equal sections. Take one section, covering the other five. Roll dough in your palm to form a round ball, then press to flatten it. Dust it with flour.

3. Feed dough through the flattening rollers to thin out dough, from the widest setting to the thinnest setting. Fold dough in half after going through each setting.

4. When dough is fed through the thinnest setting, a very thin sheet will come out. Lay sheet on table and dust it generously with cornstarch. Cover with a towel. Prepare the other sheets in the same manner.

5. Cut sheets as in step 7 above.

CRISP CURRIED CHICKEN CRESCENTS

Makes about 16

These delicious crescents not only are easy to make but also can be prepared in advance. They are excellent as an appetizer or as lunch with a soup. You may also use cooked turkey, beef, pork, or ham to substitute for the chicken breasts.

PREPARATION OF INGREDIENTS

CHICKEN MIXTURE (mix in a bowl)†

> *1½ boned skinless chicken breasts: cut into pea-sized pieces (to make 1 cup)*
> *about ⅓ egg white*
> *2 teaspoons cornstarch*

3 tablespoons lard or shortening for stir-frying
⅓ cup chopped onion
2 scallions: cut into pea-sized pieces, including some green
2 tablespoons flour
⅓ cup water

SAUCE MIXTURE (mix in a bowl)†

> *¼ teaspoon five-fragrance powder*
> *2 teaspoons curry powder*
> *½ teaspoon sugar*
> *¼ teaspoon salt*
> *⅛ teaspoon ground pepper*
> *2 teaspoons thin soy sauce*
> *2 teaspoons sherry*

¼ cup snipped parsley
about 16 slices soft white bread (Wonder Bread works perfectly): cut off crusts, roll bread with rolling pin until thin, cover with a damp towel
1 to 2 egg yolks: put in a bowl
oil for deep-frying
Soy-Vinegar Dip (page 174; optional)

DIRECTIONS FOR COOKING

1. Blanch chicken mixture in water (see page 192). Set aside.
2. Heat wok over medium heat, add lard or shortening, and spread to grease wok. Drop in onion and scallions. Stir and cook for several seconds; remove from wok and let oil drip back into wok.
3. Keeping wok hot over medium heat, drop in flour and stir immediately, splash in the water, and stir quickly to mix well (it

forms a thick mass). Turn off heat. Add sauce mixture and mix well. Add blanched chicken, onions, scallions, and parsley. Mix filling and put in a bowl to cool in refrigerator.

4. Put a heaping tablespoon of filling in the center of a piece of bread; brush egg yolk around edges; fold bread in half; pinch to seal tightly. Trim edges with scissors to form crescents, and put between linen towels. Make the others in the same manner.

5. Heat oil to deep-fry temperature (375 degrees). Deep-fry crescents to golden brown. Drain on paper towels. Serve hot with dip or without.

Note: Crescents can be made a day or two in advance up through step 4; refrigerate or freeze (separate each with wax paper) before deep-frying. Fried crescents also can be kept in low or warm oven for at least 30 minutes.

MOCK OYSTER PUFFS

(DEEP-FRIED EGGPLANT PUFFS)

Makes about 24

Many monasteries in China serve meals—all vegetable dishes, of course. But many of their vegetable dishes are contrived to imitate seafood or meat. For in the olden days, the rich, the noble, and even the emperor went to spend a day or two in a monastery. One could not expect that an emperor would be happy to chew on a carrot or sunflower seed. Therefore, the monks delighted their honorable guest with bean curd skins pressed together and seasoned to taste like roasted duck. A high-gluten dough is made to resemble abalone, and eggplant fried to imitate the oyster. So, for centuries, the monasteries in China have had their own cuisine.

These crisp, tasty puffs are popular in the monasteries but on the streets as well. We love to eat them as snacks, smeared with chili sauce or dipped in soy-vinegar. They also make a splendid appetizer.

PREPARATION OF INGREDIENTS

about 1 pound of eggplant (preferably small ones): unpeeled, cut into
 ¼-inch thin rounds
2 tablespoons thin soy sauce
1 teaspoon five-fragrance powder (optional)
Chef's Puff-Crisp Batter (page 6)
oil for deep frying

SOY-VINEGAR DIP (mix in a small serving bowl)†

 4 tablespoons Chinese red vinegar
 2 tablespoons black soy sauce

a small dish of Chinese chili sauce or Tabasco sauce (optional)

DIRECTIONS FOR COOKING

1. In a bowl, marinate eggplant rounds with soy sauce and optional five-fragrance powder for about 5 minutes. Discard sauce.

2. Lay eggplant rounds on a large tray and allow to drain for about 2 hours. Discard liquid. Pat dry with towels.

3. Heat oil to deep-fry temperature (375 degrees). Dip eggplant rounds in batter and deep-fry, a few at a time, until golden brown. Drain on paper towels. They can be kept in a low oven for about 30 minutes. Serve hot with dip or sauce.

CHINESE FLAKY PASTRY WITH
THREE FILLINGS

Makes about 16

These pastries can be filled and fried in advance. They can also be frozen after cooking. Reheat by placing frozen pastry on a cookie sheet in a 350-degree oven for about 20 minutes or until they are thoroughly heated. They make an elegant lunch with a soup, or a tea snack or appetizer. For those who love sweet pastry, I also include two sweet fillings.

PREPARATION OF INGREDIENTS

Basic Chinese Flaky Pastry (page 8)

FILLING (mix in a bowl)†

> *1 cup minced Chinese ham, or Smithfield ham, sandwich ham, or half-crisp bacon*
> *1 cup scallions, in pea-sized pieces, including some green*

About 4 cups oil for deep-frying

DIRECTIONS FOR COOKING

1. Prepare puff pastry as in recipe. Spoon about 2 heaping teaspoons of filling in the center of a circle, and top with another circle to make a sandwich. Pinch edges together to seal; then crimp edges. Cover with damp kitchen towel. Make others in the same manner. Keep refrigerated until ready to be fried.

2. Heat oil to deep-fry temperature (375 degrees). Deep-fry puffs, a few at a time, to golden brown, turning from time to time. Drain on paper towels. Serve hot or warm.

Note: If sandwich ham or bacon is used in the filling, add ¾ teaspoon salt, or to taste.

ALTERNATE SWEET FILLING I

   1 can (18 ounces) sweet red bean paste

ALTERNATE SWEET FILLING 2 (mix in a bowl)

   *½ cup sesame seeds: roast in ungreased pot over low heat until
      golden brown, crack slightly with a nut grinder or rolling pin
   ½ cup sugar
   1 cup sweetened flaked coconut*

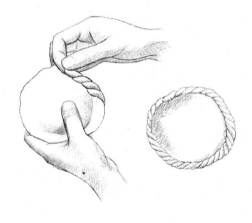

VEGETARIAN SPRING ROLLS

Makes 20

Numbers of my nephews and nieces are vegetarians, and so are children of my friends. A few are dead serious, but the rest are part-timers; that means they make compromises on Thanksgiving, Christmas, and special occasions. Our thirteen-year-old daughter has been considering joining the vegetarians even though she is not fond of vegetables because she feels sorry for the animals. But she loves crispy food, especially spring rolls. For her and for other vegetarians, this recipe and the following one were put together. They not only contain protein but also are full of wonderful flavor, to be enjoyed by carnivores as well as herbivores.

As for myself, I would rather live fifty years tasting the crisp and fragrant skin of Peking duck and juicy pork than one hundred and twenty years eating like a rabbit. I thumbed through the Old Testament, and found that even God enjoyed a lamb. Good; I don't want to feel guilty every time I bite into a piece of crisp chicken. Now they tell me that even plants have feeling. When we bite into a zucchini, it cries. Next time I see the Almighty, I will ask him or her to make me into a tall tree, eating wind and drinking dew.

PREPARATION OF INGREDIENTS

2 tablespoons oil or shortening to stir-fry
½ cup shredded leeks or scallions, in 1½-inch length, including some green
6 large Chinese dried mushrooms: soak in hot water until spongy, discard stems, shred caps

SHRIMP MIXTURE (mix in a bowl, refrigerate until use)†

½ pound medium-sized fresh shrimp: peel, devein, rinse in running cold water, pat dry, cut each in half lengthwise
1 teaspoon cornstarch
1 teaspoon sherry

½ *egg white*

about ¾ pound zucchini: cut into ¼-inch-thick rounds, then cut rounds in matchstick strips—but do not shred—by hand or in food processor (to make 3 cups)
1 cup bamboo shoots cut in matchstick strips: rinse thoroughly in cold water, drain
2 ounces bean thread noodles: soak in hot tap water for about 5 minutes to soften, drain in colander, shorten a little with a pair of scissors

SAUCE MIXTURE (mix in bowl)†

> ½ *teaspoon five-fragrance powder*
> *1 teaspoon salt*
> ½ *teaspoon sugar*
> *2 teaspoons cornstarch*
> *2 tablespoons mushroom soy or black soy sauce*
> *2 tablespoons dry sherry*

20 spring roll skins (egg roll skins may be used)
2 egg yolks for sealing spring rolls (for egg roll skins, use water to seal)
oil for pan-frying
Soy-Vinegar Dip, Mustard-Oil Dip, or Plum Sauce Dip (see recipes) (choose one or two you prefer)
a small dish of Chinese chili sauce or Tabasco sauce (optional)

DIRECTIONS FOR COOKING

1. Heat wok over high heat. Add oil or shortening and spread it with spatula. When it is hot, drop in leeks or scallions and mushrooms, and stir-fry for about 15 seconds. Add shrimp mixture; stir and cook for several seconds (shrimp should be only half-cooked). Add zucchini, bamboo shoots, and noodles. Stir-fry for about 10 seconds. Stir in sauce mixture; toss to mix well; turn off heat. (Since this is a filling which will be wrapped and fried, it is preferable that the shrimp be undercooked and the zucchini half-cooked but still green.) Transfer the entire contents to a large uncovered tray and cool in refrigerator until it is no longer warm to touch.†

2. Put about 2 heaping tablespoons of filling on a spring roll skin or egg roll skin. Cover the remaining skins with linen towel to

keep from drying out. Wrap as illustrated, and seal with egg yolk. If egg roll skins are used, seal with water.

3. In a large heavy skillet, add enough oil to reach about halfway up the rolls. Heat oil over medium heat. When oil is hot, add enough rolls to cover bottom of skillet. Pan-fry rolls, turning from time to time, until golden brown. Roll them on paper towels to drain off oil. Serve hot with dips and a sauce if desired.

Notes: You may freeze spring rolls up to Step 3. Put them on trays. Separate each layer with wax paper to prevent sticking if they are stacked. Cover with double layers of foil and seal tightly. Do not allow them to thaw, but pan-fry while they are still frozen. The oil temperature should be moderate, so that the filling can be heated thoroughly.

These delicious spring rolls are not for strict vegetarians, since shrimp is used in the filling.

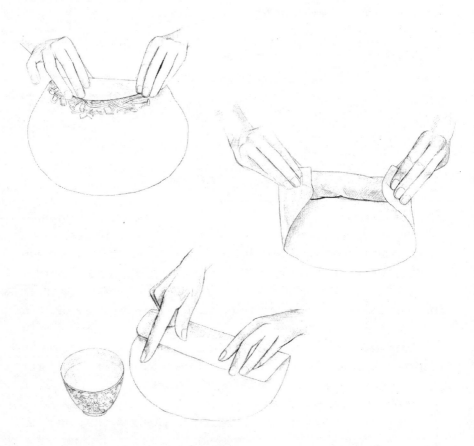

BUDDHIST SPRING ROLLS

Makes 20

PREPARATION OF INGREDIENTS

3 tablespoons oil
3 eggs: beat with ¼ teaspoon salt
½ cup shredded leeks or scallions in 1½-inch length, including some green
8 large Chinese dried mushrooms: soak in hot water until spongy, discard stems, cut caps in thin strips
2 pieces five-fragrance bean curd (page 196), cut in thin strips
2 cups packed Chinese celery cabbage, cut in thin strips crosswise
1 cup canned bamboo shoots cut in matchstick strips: rinse thoroughly in cold water, drain
8 water chestnuts: shred
2 tablespoons dried cloud ears (tree mushrooms): soak in hot water until soft and fully expanded, tear each in 4 pieces, discard any tough parts
1 ounce bean thread noodles: soak in hot water for about 5 minutes to soften, drain in colander, shorten a little with a pair of scissors

SAUCE MIXTURE (mix in a bowl)†

  ½ teaspoon salt
  1 teaspoon sugar
  ⅛ teaspoon ground pepper

continued

2 tablespoons mushroom soy or black soy sauce
1 tablespoon sherry
1 teaspoon sesame seed oil

20 spring roll skins (or egg roll skins)
2 egg yolks for sealing spring roll skins (for egg roll skins, use water to seal)
oil for pan-frying
Soy-Vinegar Dip, Mustard-Oil Dip, Chinese chili sauce, or Plum Sauce Dip (see recipes) (choose one or two you prefer)

DIRECTIONS FOR COOKING

1. Heat wok over medium-low heat. Add 2 tablespoons of the oil. When oil is hot, pour in eggs. Spread eggs by tilting and rotating wok. When eggs begin to set around the edge, lift cooked edge and allow uncooked eggs to run under. Repeat this procedure until eggs are cooked but still moist. Put on a chopping board and cut into sugar-cube-sized chunks. Set aside.

2. Heat wok over medium-high heat. Heat the remaining 1 tablespoon oil and spread with spatula. When oil is hot, drop in leeks or scallions and mushrooms and stir-fry for about 10 seconds; add bean curd, celery cabbage, bamboo shoots, water chestnuts, and cloud ears. Stir-fry for about a minute. Stir in sauce mixture and mix well. Add bean thread noodles and egg chunks. Toss and stir to mix well. Turn off heat. Transfer the entire contents to a large tray, uncovered, and cool in refrigerator until it is no longer warm to touch.

3. Put about 2 heaping tablespoons of filling on a spring roll skin (or egg roll skin). Cover the remaining skins with linen towel to keep from drying out. Wrap as illustrated (page 22) and seal with egg yolks. If egg roll skins are used, seal with water.

4. In a large heavy skillet, add enough oil to reach about halfway up the rolls. Heat oil over medium heat. When oil is hot, add enough rolls to cover bottom of skillet. Pan-fry rolls, turning from time to time, until golden brown. Roll on paper towels to drain off oil. Serve hot with one or two of the dips you choose.

CRISP BEAN CURD PUFFS

Makes 20 to 24

PREPARATION OF INGREDIENTS

10 to 12 fried bean curd puffs: cut each diagonally in half to make triangles; turn each triangle inside out, and pinch off the spongelike center

STUFFING (mix in a bowl, refrigerate until use)†

8 ounces ground pork
6 ounces fresh shrimp: shell, devein, rinse in cold water, pat dry, cut into peanut-sized pieces
5 Chinese dried mushrooms: soak in hot water until spongy, squeeze off water, discard stems, mince caps
4 water chestnuts: mince into rice-sized pieces
2 scallions: mince, including some green
1 egg: beat until slightly foamy
¼ teaspoon salt
¼ teaspoon sugar
⅛ teaspoon ground pepper
1 tablespoon thin soy sauce

about 2 tablespoons flour for dredging
4 cups oil for deep-frying
Soy-Vinegar Dip (page 174): put in a small serving bowl

DIRECTIONS FOR COOKING

1. Fill each triangle generously with stuffing, and dredge the meat edge with flour.

2. Heat oil in wok over high heat to deep-fry temperature (375 degrees). Deep-fry stuffed puffs with meat side up until the bottoms are crisp. Then turn meat sides down and deep-fry until they are golden brown (about 7 minutes total cooking time). Drain puffs. Put on a serving plate. Serve hot with dip.

CRISP COUNTRY ROLLS

Makes 8 rolls; serves 6 to 8 as snack or as an appetizer

PREPARATION OF INGREDIENTS

2 tablespoons oil
2 Chinese pork sausages: cut into small pieces
*3 tablespoons dried shrimp: wash and soak in hot water until soft, chop
    into small pieces*
*10 Chinese dried mushrooms: soak in hot water until spongy, discard
    stems, shred caps*
*1 pound sah goh or 1¼ pounds fresh water chestnuts: peel, cut into
    matchstick strips or small strips if water chestnuts are used*
1¼ teaspoons salt
1 tablespoon thin soy sauce
1 teaspoon five-fragrance powder

BATTER

> *1¼ cups plus 1 tablespoon cold water*
> *1 teaspoon salt*
> *2 teaspoons baking powder*
> *1½ cups all-purpose flour*
> *½ cup cornstarch*
> *1 tablespoon oil*

2 bean curd skins (each 24 inches in diameter): cut each into quarters
oil for deep-frying
*Soy-Vinegar Dip (page 174) and a small bowl of Chinese chili sauce or
    Tabasco sauce*

DIRECTIONS FOR COOKING

1. Heat wok hot over high heat. Swirl in oil. When oil is hot, drop in sausages and stir-fry until pieces sizzle. Add shrimp and stir to cook for about 20 seconds; stir in mushrooms and stir to cook for another 20 seconds. Add sah goh, 1¼ teaspoons salt, and soy sauce. Stir-fry until sah goh just begins to soften. If water

chestnuts are used, cook briefly. Turn off heat. Add five-fragrance powder, and mix well. Keep the filling in the refrigerator until it is thoroughly cool.†

2. Put water, 1 teaspoon salt, and baking powder in a mixing bowl. Stir in flour and cornstarch gradually and mix with an eggbeater until smooth. Stir in 1 tablespoon oil, and mix thoroughly. Pour batter in a roasting pan. Cover with a damp cloth.

3. Cover quartered bean curd skins with wet cloth to moisten them. Keep them covered.

4. When bean curd skins are softened, divide the filling into 8 portions and make a row of filling along the wide side of each skin. Wrap as illustrated. Moisten edges with batter to seal. Cover with a damp cloth.

5. Heat oil over medium-high heat to deep-fry temperature (375 degrees). Put rolls in batter to coat evenly; put in oil. Deep-fry rolls, two at a time, until golden brown. Drain and roll on paper towels. Cut each with scissors into three sections. Serve hot or at room temperature with dip and sauce.

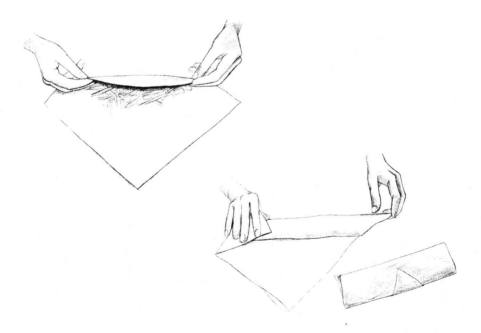

CURRIED BEEF AND MUSHROOM TURNOVERS

Makes about 26

PREPARATION OF INGREDIENTS

3 tablespoons lard or shortening for stir-frying
½ cup chopped onion
½ cup sliced fresh mushrooms

BEEF MIXTURE (mix in a bowl)†

> *½ pound coarsely ground beef or pork (you may use food processor)*
> *¼ teaspoon baking soda (if beef is used)*
> *2 teaspoons cornstarch*
> *1 tablespoon sherry*
> *2 teaspoons sesame oil*
> *2 teaspoons black soy sauce (not double black soy sauce)*

SEASONINGS (put in a bowl)†

> *2 teaspoons curry powder*
> *⅛ teaspoon cayenne pepper*
> *¼ teaspoon salt*
> *¼ cup snipped parsley*

Basic Chinese Flaky Pastry (page 8)
oil for deep-frying

DIRECTIONS FOR COOKING

1. Heat wok hot over medium heat. Add lard or shortening and spread with a spatula. Drop in onion and mushrooms. Stir and cook until onion turns clear; add beef mixture. Stir-fry until beef is no longer red. Turn off heat. Add seasonings and mix well; put in refrigerator to cool.†

2. Prepare flaky pastry as in recipe. Spoon about 2 heaping teaspoons of filling in the center of a pastry circle. Fold circle in half to form a half-moon. Pinch edges tightly together to seal. Then crimp edges. Cover with a damp kitchen towel. Make the others in the same manner.

3. Deep-fry turnovers to golden brown. Drain on paper towels. Serve hot or warm.

Notes: Fried turnovers can be frozen in foil. Thaw and reheat uncovered in a 350-degree oven for about 15 minutes or until crisp and heated through.

Also, you may use about 16 slices of soft white bread as wrappers, as in the recipe for Crisp Curried Chicken Crescents (see page 14). Roll bread slices and seal turnovers with egg yolk as in that recipe.

TURNIP AND SAUSAGE TURNOVERS

Makes about 26

PREPARATION OF INGREDIENTS

1 tablespoon oil
4 Chinese pork sausages: cut into pea-sized pieces
1 pound Chinese white turnip: peel, cut into matchstick strips

SEASONINGS (put in a bowl)†

> *½ cup chopped scallions, including some green*
> *1 teaspoon salt*
> *½ teaspoon sugar*
> *½ teaspoon five-fragrance powder*
> *⅛ teaspoon ground white pepper*
> *2 teaspoons sesame oil*

Basic Chinese Flaky Pastry (page 8)
oil for deep-frying

DIRECTIONS FOR COOKING

1. Heat wok hot over medium-high heat. Swirl in 1 tablespoon oil. Add sausages; stir and cook until they sizzle. Add turnip; stir-fry until it becomes limp and soft. Add seasonings and mix well. Turn off heat. Put in a bowl, and cool in refrigerator before use.

2. Prepare flaky pastry as in recipe. Spoon about 2 tablespoons

of filling in the center of the circle. Fold circle in half to form a half-moon. Pinch edges tightly together to seal. Then crimp edges. Put between kitchen towels. Make the others in the same manner.

3. Deep-fry turnovers to golden brown. Drain on paper towels. Serve hot or warm.

Note: Fried turnovers can be frozen in foil. Thaw and reheat uncovered in a 350-degree oven for about 15 minutes or until crisp and heated through.

SAVORY TARO TURNOVERS

Makes 20 to 24

Taro, a starchy tuber with dusty rough brown skin, comes in many sizes and varieties.

The best kind is large, big as a coconut; the flesh inside is dry, white, and lined with feathery purple strands. The flesh is fragrant after it is cooked, fluffy if mashed. The Chinese call this kind, best for making pastry, "the fragrant taro." Most Chinese grocery stores have one or two taros cut open, so that the customers can see the flesh inside.

I suggest that you shop with the Shopping List in this book, for I have put in the Chinese name of the best kind of taro so that Chinese grocers will know what you want. Of course, go to a reliable grocer. Taro is also available in some Spanish stores. Use it within a week.

PREPARATION OF INGREDIENTS

2½ pounds taro: peel, cut into ¼-inch slices, steam for 20 minutes or
  until done
½ cup wheat starch (see page 216)
½ cup boiling water
9 tablespoons lard or shortening
2 tablespoons sugar
½ teaspoon salt

FILLING

    8 Chinese mushrooms: soak in hot water until soft, discard stems,
       cut caps in small pieces
    ½ pound lean pork, cut in pea-sized pieces
    ⅓ cup minced bamboo shoots (rinse in cold water before mincing)
    6 ounces fresh shrimp: shell, devein, rinse in cold water, dry, cut
       into pea-sized pieces

SAUCE MIXTURE (mix in a bowl)†

    ¾ teaspoon salt
    ½ teaspoon sugar
    ⅛ teaspoon ground pepper
    2 teaspoons cornstarch
    1 tablespoon black soy sauce
    2 tablespoons sherry

2 hard-boiled eggs: peel and mince
¼ cup scallions in pea-sized pieces, including some green
about ½ cup wheat starch for dusting and coating turnovers
oil for deep-frying

DIRECTIONS FOR COOKING

   1. Put steamed taro in a large mixing bowl and mash by hand as
you would mash potatoes; discard hard pieces. (You may mash it
in a food processor.)
   2. In a medium-sized mixing bowl, place ½ cup wheat starch

and make a well. Pour in boiling water and stir quickly, then knead into a soft dough.

3. Combine mashed taro, dough, 6 tablespoons of the lard or shortening, sugar, and salt together, and knead by hand until thoroughly mixed. Cover and put taro dough aside for further use.

4. Heat and spread the remaining 3 tablespoons lard or shortening in wok. Drop in mushrooms, and stir and cook for about 10 seconds. Add pork, and stir-fry until no longer pink. Add bamboo shoots and shrimp; stir-fry until shrimp is half-cooked. Stir in sauce mixture. When sauce is thickened, turn off heat; add minced eggs and scallions; mix well. Put filling in a bowl to cool in refrigerator.

5. Dust working surface with wheat starch. Take a handful of taro dough, about as big as a lemon, and roll into a round ball. With a rolling pin, gently roll ball out into a circle about ¼ inch thick. (If dough is rolled too thin, it will burst while deep-frying.) Put 1 to 2 tablespoons filling in the center of the circle. Fold circle in half and pinch edges tightly together. Coat turnover with wheat starch and put aside. Make the remaining turnovers in the same manner.

6. Heat oil in wok. The oil temperature should not be too hot; otherwise turnovers will burst open. Test oil by dipping a wooden chopstick or wooden spoon in oil; it should just sizzle slightly. Slide turnovers into oil, a few at a time, and deep-fry at moderate temperature until golden brown. Gently remove from oil (do not use tongs or anything that would squeeze or puncture turnovers) to drain on paper towels. They can be kept in a 150-degree oven for about 30 minutes.

Note: Taro turnovers can be cooked in advance. Reheat in 350-degree oven for 15 minutes or until crisp and hot.

SAVORY SESAME SCALLION BISCUITS

Makes about 16

Do not pass over this recipe because of the simplicity of the ingredients. These delicious crisp and fragrant small cakes make wonderful snacks or appetizers.

PREPARATION OF INGREDIENTS

DOUGH

> *2 cups all-purpose flour*
> *2 teaspoons salt*
> *½ teaspoon sugar*
> *¼ cup oil*
> *⅓ cup cold water*

FILLING (mix in a bowl)†

> *⅔ cup chopped scallions, including some green*
> *3 ounces pork fat: mince to make ⅔ cup (easier if you freeze it first)*
> *1½ teaspoons salt*

½ cup white sesame seeds
oil for pan-frying

DIRECTIONS FOR COOKING

1. In a mixing bowl, combine flour, 2 teaspoons salt and sugar; stir in oil and water. Knead until it forms a ball. Put dough on a floured surface and knead until smooth. (You may do this step in a food processor.)

2. Roll dough into a long sausage, and cut it into 16 equal portions. Roll each portion into a round ball; keep them in a plastic bag to prevent drying.

3. Roll one of the balls into a paper-thin pancake; sprinkle about 2 teaspoons of filling on it, and gently rub pork fat on

pancake to grease it evenly. Roll pancake tightly into a thin long sausage. Pinch both ends to seal in scallions. Coil sausage into a round biscuit. Flatten biscuit with a rolling pin to make it thinner. (No harm is done if some scallions come out from dough.) Moisten biscuit on both sides with water. Press biscuit on sesame seeds to coat both sides. Put biscuit between kitchen towels. Make the others in the same manner.

4. Pour enough oil in a skillet to cover its bottom by about ½ inch. Heat oil over medium-low heat until it is moderately hot. Pan-fry scallion biscuit until all sides are golden brown. Drain on paper towels. Serve hot. They can be kept in a warm oven for about 30 minutes.

FIVE-FRAGRANCE FRITTERS

Makes about 18

PREPARATION OF INGREDIENTS

1 pound eggplant or zucchini: cut into thin rounds, then shred rounds into
thin strips—do not use food processor
3 eggs, beaten
½ teaspoon salt
½ teaspoon sugar
1 ½ teaspoons five-fragrance powder
2 tablespoons thin soy sauce
1 cup all-purpose flour
½ cup chopped scallions, including some green
oil for pan-frying
Soy-Vinegar Dip (page 174) and a small bowl of Chinese chili sauce or
Tabasco sauce (optional)

DIRECTIONS FOR COOKING

1. In a mixing bowl, combine the above ingredients except the oil and dip. The mixture is thick; allow it to stand for about 30 minutes or until it becomes thinner. (This mixture can be prepared hours in advance.)

2. Heat a large skillet over medium-low heat. Add enough oil to cover bottom of skillet. When oil is hot, ladle tablespoonfuls of the mixture onto the skillet; pan-fry fritters, a few at a time, over medium-low heat until both sides are golden brown and edges are crisp. While cooking, press fritters occasionally with spatula to thin them; add more oil when it is needed. Transfer them to a wire rack, then place rack with fritters on a cookie sheet, and put in a 350-degree oven until the rest are cooked. (A 350-degree oven will keep the fritters hot and crisp for about 20 minutes; beyond that time they might become dry. A 300-degree or lower oven will keep them hot longer—but softer. But they are *all* good.) Serve hot with dip.

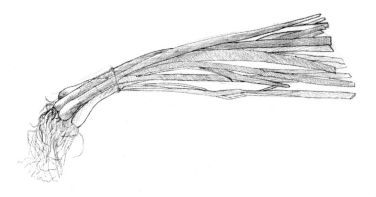

CHUNG YAO BING

(CRISP SCALLION CAKES)

Makes six 10-inch round crepes

These crisp savory cakes are one of the most loved foods among the Chinese; and no Westerner can forget them once they have tasted them. It is almost magical when a few humble ingredients—flour, scallions and lard—can create such a treat. Though originally it was a Shanghai specialty, you may find it frying at street stalls in Peking and Taiwan, served in Hong Kong restaurants and even in Chinatowns.

The ingredients seem to resemble those of a couple of other recipes in this book, but actually there is no resemblance in flavor, appearance or character. However, all reflect the humble genius of the Chinese cooks for transforming the simple into the delectable.

PREPARATION OF INGREDIENTS

4 cups all-purpose flour
2 cups water
1 tablespoon salt
6 tablespoons lard or shortening
1 ¼ cups chopped scallions, in pea-sized pieces, including some green
about ½ cup oil for pan-frying

DIRECTIONS FOR COOKING

1. In a mixing bowl, combine flour and water. Turn dough onto a floured surface, and knead until smooth. Cut dough into two portions and roll each portion into a thick sausage. Cut each sausage into three equal parts. (Now altogether you have six pieces of dough.) Roll each piece of dough into a round ball, and put them under a damp kitchen towel to prevent them from drying.

2. Dust rolling pin and working surface with flour. Roll a ball of dough into a big thin pancake (about 11 to 12 inches in diameter.) Sprinkle ½ teaspoon salt evenly on pancake, and with your fingers spread 1 tablespoon of lard or shortening on each pancake evenly; then sprinkle each with about 3 tablespoons of scallions. Roll each pancake into a sausage as you would roll up a jelly roll. Pick up the dough sausage and twist it like a rope, then hold it upright with one end on the table and press the top end straight down to the bottom end to form a round cake. Dust cake with a little flour and roll it into a thin cake about 10 inches across. Prepare the others in same manner. Put cakes between wax paper.

3. Heat a large skillet and pour in enough oil to cover the bottom generously. When oil is hot, put in a scallion cake. Pan-fry each cake over medium heat until both sides are golden brown. Drain on paper towels. They can be kept hot in a 200-degree oven. Cut cakes into big slices. Serve hot.

PEASANT PANCAKES

Makes about 24; serves 4 as a meal

PREPARATION OF INGREDIENTS

1 cup all-purpose flour
1 cup chicken broth
1 Chinese pork sausage (or ¼ cup ground pork): cut into pea-sized pieces
½ cup chopped scallions, including some green
½ cup chopped water chestnuts, in rice-sized pieces
½ cup chopped fresh shrimp, in pea-sized pieces
¼ teaspoon salt
¼ teaspoon sugar
½ teaspoon baking powder
¼ teaspoon ground pepper
¼ teaspoon cayenne pepper (optional)
about ⅓ cup oil for pan-frying
Soy-Vinegar Dip (page 174)

DIRECTIONS FOR COOKING

1. In a mixing bowl, beat flour and broth with a hand whisk or an eggbeater to a smooth batter. Stir in remaining ingredients except the oil for pan-frying and the dip. Mix well.

2. Heat skillet over medium heat. Add enough oil to cover bottom of skillet. When oil is hot, ladle about 2 tablespoons of batter for each pancake into skillet. Pan-fry pancakes until crisp and golden brown. Drain on paper towels. Serve hot with or without dip.

Note: *Batter can be prepared a day in advance; refrigerate until ready to use. Cooked pancakes can be placed in a low oven to keep warm.*

FRAGRANT TARO CRISP FRITTERS

Makes about 20

PREPARATION OF INGREDIENTS

about 1 ¼ pounds taro (see page 30)
⅓ cup wheat starch (see page 216)
¼ cup boiling water
6 ounces shrimp: shell, devein, rinse in cold water, pat dry, cut into
  pea-sized pieces
4 ounces Chinese Barbecued Pork (page 118): cut into small pieces
6 Chinese dried mushrooms: soak in hot water until spongy, discard
  stems, cut caps into small pieces
⅓ cup chopped scallions, including some green
⅛ teaspoon ground pepper
½ teaspoon salt
1 teaspoon sugar
¼ teaspoon five-fragrance powder
1 tablespoon thin soy sauce
1 tablespoon sesame oil
about ⅓ cup oil for pan-frying

DIRECTIONS FOR COOKING

1. Peel taro, cut into ½-inch slices; steam until soft, mash, and put aside.

2. Put wheat starch in a mixing bowl and make a well; pour in all the boiling water and stir quickly with a spoon. Knead and form into a soft dough.

3. Combine dough, mashed taro, and the remaining ingredients except oil for pan-frying. Knead to mix well. (You may prepare it up to this point a day or two in advance. Cover and refrigerate until use.)

4. Form mixture into small fritters. Pan-fry in small amount of oil until both sides are golden brown. Drain on paper towels. Serve hot. Taro fritters can be kept in a warm oven for about 30 minutes or more.

STEAMED DIM SUM

(Steamed Delicacies and Appetizers)

CHIAOTSES, PEKING STYLE

(BASIC STEAMED CRESCENTS, TWO KINDS OF FILLING)

Makes 24

Chiaotses, these small meat-filled crescents, are one of the most popular foods in the regions of Peking, Shanghai, Szechwan, and Hunan. Like the sandwiches of the West, they are frequently prepared at home or eaten in restaurants as snacks as well as meals.

Chiaotse skins are a little thicker and sturdier than the Cantonese wonton. And their fillings are more meaty, robust with juicy minced pork and scallions, pork with chopped Chinese cabbage, beef, or mutton. They are either steamed or boiled, or fried to be crusty on one side.

Chiaotses are served mostly by the dozen; the steamed ones are snuggled in bamboo steamer trays; the boiled ones gleam in tasty soup; and the fried ones show off by lying in rows on the plate with their crusty sides up.

Accompany them with a cup of tea, or a bowl of soup, and a bottle of good Chinese beer (we have great beer), and no one can leave the table contented without consuming a dozen chiaotses.

They are not only an excellent snack for before or after the theater but also a hearty meal that does not strain one's purse. And they are even cheaper if prepared at home.

When I was growing up in China, most women, children, and even men learned to make chiaotses. It was always a festive activity in my family. Encircling the big round dining table we all sat: grandmother, mother, our maids Noble Face and Obedience, and often a few distant relatives we called uncle and aunt but knew as "eating guests," who needed a place to eat and stay. Sometimes we were joined by Old Chan, my father's helper from Shantung Province, the best chiaotse maker we had ever known.

Busy hands and bumping shoulders hovered over the large bowl of filling, while the gong-voices of Grandmother and Noble Face clashed with the deafening sound of Old Chan's cleaver pounding on the meat.

Old Chan was immense, with a shaved head; with his northern dialect, he was forever branded a stranger in the southern cities of Canton and Hong Kong. He was not old, but in his forties when my father gave him a coat and a small amount of money just before the Japanese war. He stood shivering and starving at the door of a Shanghai hotel where my father stayed. And when he was brought home my mother was not surprised, for father never failed to believe a sad story of life even though he had heard it many times. Unlike some others, Old Chan was helpful in the household and feverishly loyal to father. And mother could not bear to set him astray.

He was once an army cook—actually for a warlord, we believed. And when he was not traveling with father on business he loved to make chiaotses and noodles. Grandmother was usually the one to prepare the dough, but we much preferred Old Chan. He twisted and stretched the dough in midair and sometimes snaked it around our necks.

He never used a rolling pin, because a good chiaotse maker was most proud of showing off his fast hands. First, he would pinch off a small piece of dough, the size of a walnut, and roll it between his palms to round it. Then he placed the round dough between his thumbs and all eight fingertips. Like a wheel spinning at high speed, his fingers rotated the dough clockwise until it became an even, thin round bowl to hold the filling. Then the chiaotse was filled and pleated, and its thin edges were pinched together to form a seal. And a delicate chiaotse resembling a dainty silk purse was placed on a tray.

The children were all accepted at the preparation table, as long as our hands were not too dirty and our breaths were not too wet. When our chiaotses looked like some sleeping dinosaurs, Old Chan would announce, "A chiaotse reflects one's artistic nature!" Then our hands hurried to explore "artistic nature," creating more half-awake chiaotse dinosaurs.

When Old Chan was in the right mood—and he seldom was not when there was an audience—he would bellow his favorite songs of his home, the North. They tended to be about a maiden far away and her beautiful black eyes and a camel song that was full of the sound of Hey! Ah! Hey! Since the words made no sense to us then, we called them "the cow dung songs"; but we loved to echo loudly, Hey! Ah! Hey! Excited by the commotion, our little twin sisters would run gurgling around the table.

Except for mother's composed face and the constrained politeness of the "eating guests," Old Chan might have been a genie reveling in a goblin's lair.

The chiaotse-making process would be much delayed if Old Chan was wound up to his Peking Opera mood. In the middle of the room, he would sing in a shrilling lady's voice, and like a bear on tiptoe imitate her willowy steps, a weeping heroine lamenting her bygone lover. And to the children's delight he would somersault and peer about, acting our famous monkey saint, Shu Woo Tung. Then no one could make chiaotses. We doubled up, stomachs aching in uncontrollable laughter.

When, finally, the piping hot juicy chiaotses were served, Old Chan would claim his share—three dozen and sometimes more. So when he was lazy my father called him "Shantung Rice Bucket"; when he talked too much, "Shantung Cannon." Twenty-five years ago I said, "See you again" to Old Chan. Like many others that I did not then realize, it was a last goodbye.

Now I make dainty chiaotses with flying fingers like Old Chan, and sing the songs of the camel and maiden that now I understand—a heart's longing for home, even after a willing goodbye.

PREPARATION OF INGREDIENTS

CHIAOTSE SKINS

> *2 cups all-purpose flour*
> *¼ teaspoon salt*
> *¾ cup boiling water*

BASIC FILLING (stir filling vigorously with chopsticks or wooden spoon by hand for about a minute to make it sticky and pasty; refrigerate until use)

> *1 pound ground pork*
> *½ pound Chinese celery cabbage: separate leaves, steam for about 10 minutes or until tender; mince; put in colander and squeeze off excess water*
> *⅓ cup minced scallions, including some green*
> *½ teaspoon salt*
> *¼ teaspoon white pepper*
> *¼ teaspoon sugar*
> *2 tablespoons black soy sauce*
> *1 tablespoon sherry*

ALTERNATE FILLING (mix and stir as for Basic Filling above)

> *1 pound ground pork, beef or veal*
> *½ cup chopped scallions, including some green*
> *½ teaspoon salt*
> *½ teaspoon sugar*
> *¼ teaspoon ground pepper*
> *2 teaspoons sesame oil*
> *4 teaspoons black soy sauce*
> *1 tablespoon sherry*

Ginger-Soy-Vinegar Dip (page 174) and a dish of Chili Oil (page 170)

DIRECTIONS FOR COOKING

1. In a mixing bowl, combine flour and salt and make a well. Quickly pour in the boiling water. Stir immediately with a wooden spoon. Form hot dough into a ball.

2. Turn dough onto a floured surface and knead until smooth,

soft but not sticky. Put in a floured plastic bag to rest for about 10 minutes.

3. Roll dough into a long sausage, 1 inch in diameter, and cut it into 24 equal portions. Roll each portion to a round ball and cover with a plastic bag to keep from drying.

4. With a rolling pin, roll each ball into a thin circle. Put a heaping tablespoon of filling in the center of the circle. Fold circle into half. Pleat front edge toward its center, then pinch the pleated edge and bottom edge tightly together into a thin edge. Place chiaotse, wide bottom down, between linen towels to keep from sticking and drying. Chiaotses can be made hours in advance, but be sure to keep them refrigerated until steaming.

5. Place chiaotses on an oiled steamer tray. Cover and steam over boiling water for about 12 minutes (see steaming methods, pages 184–188). Serve hot with dip.

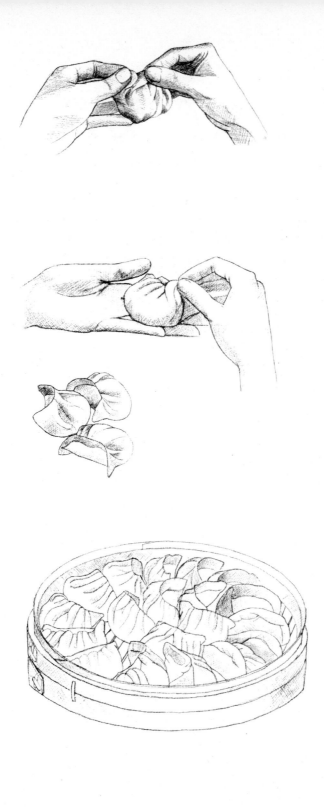

FOUR HAPPINESSES SHAO MAI

(STEAMED FOUR-COLOR STUFFED PASTRY)

Makes 24

These delicious little stuffed pastries are decorated with four cheerful colors which we call "the four happinesses": black mushrooms, yellow egg, green parsley or scallions, and reddish barbecued pork or ham. They are so finely made and beautiful that they make any party or dinner an event. Their dazzling presence expresses the cook's thoughtfulness and good wishes on the occasion, and thus enhances a happy gathering such as a birthday, graduation, wedding, or anniversary.

I suggest serving them from the bamboo steamer for lunch or a tea snack, or passing them around as an appetizer.

They can be made a day in advance, and steamed just before serving.

PREPARATION OF INGREDIENTS

1 tablespoon oil
1 egg: beat thoroughly with a pinch of salt

WRAPPERS

>*1 cup all-purpose flour*
>*1 cup cake flour (if not available, use all-purpose flour)*
>*½ teaspoon salt*
>*¾ cup boiling water*
>*1 tablespoon lard or shortening*

a handful of flour for dusting

FILLING (mix and stir in a bowl until pasty)†

>*12 ounces fresh shrimp: shell, devein, rinse in cold water, pat dry, cut into pea-sized pieces*
>*1 egg white: beat until foamy*

6 ounces ground pork
¾ cup minced bamboo shoots or water chestnuts
2 teaspoons minced fresh ginger
3 tablespoons minced scallions, including some green
¾ teaspoon salt
½ teaspoon sugar
2 teaspoons cornstarch
⅛ teaspoon ground pepper
1 tablespoon thin soy sauce
2 teaspoons sherry
2 teaspoons sesame oil

⅓ cup each of the following garnishes: chopped parsley or scallions, soaked Chinese dried mushrooms, minced Chinese Barbecued Pork (page 118) or Smithfield ham or sandwich ham
Ginger-Soy-Vinegar dip (page 172)

DIRECTIONS FOR COOKING

1. Heat a skillet or wok over medium heat, and oil the surface with 1 tablespoon oil. Swirl in the egg and spread to form a very thin pancake. When egg is set, turn to cook the other side briefly. Transfer egg pancake to a cutting board and cut into thin shreds. Put aside for later use.

2. In a mixing bowl, combine the two kinds of flour and salt. Pour in boiling water all at once and stir quickly. Mix and knead with hand to form a rough dough. Add lard or shortening and knead until dough becomes very smooth. Put in a covered bowl to rest for about 10 minutes.

3. Dust work area with flour. Roll dough into the shape of a sausage and cut it into 24 equal sections. Roll each section into a ball. Cover them to prevent drying.

4. Divide filling into 24 equal portions on a tray.

5. Use a floured rolling pin and roll each ball into a thin round wrapper 4½ to 5 inches in diameter. Put a portion of filling in the center of the wrapper, fold and wrap as illustrated, and fill the four openings with egg shreds and the garnishes. Prepare the

others in the same manner. Cover shao mai with a damp cloth. (They can be made a day in advance; refrigerate until use.)

6. Steam shao mai in an oiled steamer over high heat for about 7 minutes. Serve hot with dip.

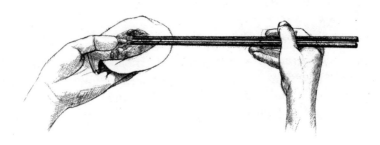

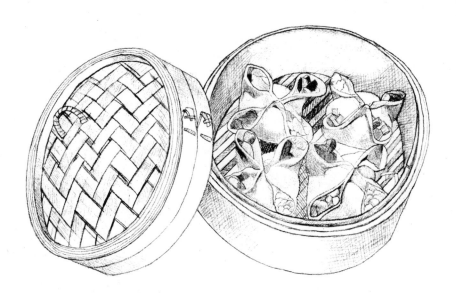

TEAHOUSE SPARERIBS IN GARLIC AND BLACK BEAN SAUCE

Serves 2 as a meal

Small dishes of steamed spareribs in various sauces are part of the dim sum dishes offered in teahouses. But many Chinese families also serve these ribs as a dinner dish, for they require little preparation and the sauce is excellent with rice.

PREPARATION OF INGREDIENTS

SPARERIB MIXTURE (mix together and marinate at least 1 hour in refrigerator)†

> 1 pound pork spareribs: ask your butcher to cut them into bite-sized pieces and trim off excess fat
> 3 tablespoons salted black beans: put in a small drainer, rinse in running hot water, drain, mash to paste.
> 1 to 2 fresh chili peppers (optional): cut into small rounds; use seeds also
> 1 small piece of dried tangerine peel (optional): soak in hot water for 10 minutes, mince (to make 2 teaspoons)
> 1 tablespoon minced garlic
> ¼ teaspoon salt
> ½ teaspoon sugar
> 2 tablespoons thin soy sauce
> 2 teaspoons sherry

2 teaspoons sesame oil
2 tablespoons chopped scallions, including some green

DIRECTIONS FOR COOKING

1. Put sparerib mixture in a 9-inch heatproof plate (a pie plate will do).
2. Steam spareribs over water for about 10 minutes. Pour in sesame oil and mix well. Transfer the whole contents to a heated serving platter; top with scallions. Serve hot with or without rice.

SPICED CHICKEN IN A PUMPKIN

Serves 6 as an appetizer

The pumpkin, which we call "southern melon," grows abundantly south of the Yangtze River. The pumpkin is considered a cheap vegetable. Except for this extraordinary one from Szechwan, there are very few dishes that put the pumpkin in the spotlight. In this dish, the chicken is spiced with Szechwan peppercorns and coated with glutinous rice, steamed, then served right from the pumpkin.

PREPARATION OF INGREDIENTS

1 fresh whole pumpkin, about 5 pounds
⅓ cup glutinous rice (see page 209)
½ teaspoon flower peppercorns
3 tablespoons water
5 tablespoons Chinese Shaohsing wine or sake

CHICKEN MIXTURE (mix and put in a shallow heatproof dish)†

1 large boned, skinless chicken breast: trim and pound with the back
of cleaver and cut into pencil-thin strips 1½ inches long
2 tablespoons Szechwan sweet bean sauce or ground bean sauce
2 tablespoons Szechwan chili bean sauce
1 tablespoon black soy sauce
1 tablespoon sugar
2 scallions: cut into pea-sized pieces, including some green
1 teaspoon minced fresh ginger root
2 tablespoons melted lard or oil

2 teaspoons sesame oil

DIRECTIONS FOR COOKING

1. Cut the top of the pumpkin about 2 to 3 inches below the base of the handle neatly, so that the top will fit tightly like a lid. Scoop out seeds and soft center. Rinse inside with hot water. Pour out water and pat dry.

2. Heat a small pot. Add the rice, and roast over medium-low heat until golden brown. Stir frequently. Add peppercorns to the hot rice and roast until they turn dark brown and aromatic. Remove from heat. Put rice and peppercorns into a plastic bag or between two pieces of cloth. Crush or roll them into a coarse powder with a rolling pin (or use an electric coffee mill or spice grinder). Place rice and peppercorn powder in a bowl, moisten mixture with 3 tablespoons water and 3 tablespoons wine, then stir and mix with the chicken mixture.†

3. Steam mixture over high heat in a heatproof dish for 15 minutes. Remove from heat and keep covered so it will stay hot.

4. At the same time, cover and steam pumpkin with lid in a big pot containing 1 inch of water for 15 minutes. (Wrap cheesecloth around pumpkin, so that it can be easily lifted out of the pot.)

5. Spoon piping hot chicken into the steamed pumpkin and pour in the remaining 2 tablespoons wine. Stir chicken to mix in wine and replace the pumpkin lid. Cover and steam chicken in the pumpkin for 20 minutes. Lift pumpkin out of pot gently. Stir sesame oil into chicken. Serve chicken hot from the pumpkin. The pumpkin is not for eating in this dish.

Note: You may substitute 1 cup of pork for the chicken. Use cutlets or boned pork chops and cut them into pencil-thin strips.

STEAMED SPICED BEEF WITH FRAGRANT RICE

Serves 6 to 8 as an appetizer

PREPARATION OF INGREDIENTS

6 tablespoons glutinous rice (see page 209)
4 tablespoons long- or short-grain rice
1 pound flank steak: cut against grain into strips 1½ inches long, ½ inch wide, and ⅓ inch thick

SAUCE MIXTURE (mix in a bowl)†

¼ teaspoon ground pepper
¼ teaspoon cayenne pepper or ground chili pepper (optional)
1 teaspoon sugar
3 tablespoons mushroom soy or black soy sauce
3 tablespoons peanut oil
1 teaspoon ginger juice (use garlic press to squeeze)
5 teaspoons Szechwan sweet bean sauce
5 teaspoons Szechwan chili bean sauce
2 tablespoons Shaohsing wine or dry sherry
2 tablespoons water

6 to 8 dried bamboo leaves or 1 large lotus leaf (optional): soak in warm
water to soften, pat dry
¼ cup chopped scallions, including some green
¼ cup chopped fresh coriander (leaves only), in a small serving bowl
flower peppercorn powder, in a small serving dish

DIRECTIONS FOR COOKING

1. Mix the two kinds of rice and roast in a small pot over low heat, stirring constantly, until they are golden brown. Put them in a plastic bag, and crush coarsely with a rolling pin. Set aside.

2. Mix crushed rice and beef in a bowl. Pour in sauce mixture and mix well. Cover and marinate for at least 30 minutes.

3. Line a 10- to 12-inch bamboo steamer tray with bamboo leaves, overlapping each other, or a lotus leaf. Spoon beef and rice mixture on top.

4. Cover and steam over high heat for 10 minutes. Stir and turn beef and rice mixture with chopsticks. Cover and steam for another 5 minutes or until rice is cooked. (Do not oversteam.) Sprinkle scallions on top. Bring coriander, Szechwan peppercorn powder, and steamer to the table. Serve hot directly from steamer with a little coriander and peppercorn powder.

Notes: *If you do not have a bamboo steamer, put beef and rice mixture in an 8-inch heatproof dish. Cover and steam (see pages 184–188).*

You may also line the bamboo steamer with washed bok choy or cabbage leaves if bamboo or lotus leaves are not available.

TEAHOUSE STEAMED STUFFED MUSHROOMS ON VEGETABLE

Makes 24

PREPARATION OF INGREDIENTS

MARINADE (mix together and marinate for about 10 minutes)

> *12 half-dollar-sized Chinese dried mushrooms: soak in hot water until spongy, discard stems, squeeze off water*
> *1 tablespoon oil*
> *1 tablespoon mushroom soy or black soy sauce*
> *1 tablespoon sherry*
> *¼ teaspoon sugar*
> *1 teaspoon minced fresh ginger root*
> *1 tablespoon minced scallion, including some green*

SHRIMP MIXTURE (combine all ingredients; beat vigorously with a wooden spoon for a minute, refrigerate until use)†

> *1 pound fresh shrimp: peel, devein, clean in running cold water, pat dry, mince by hand or by food processor, but do not allow to become too pasty*
> *2 tablespoons minced fat bacon*
> *1 egg white: beat slightly*
> *2 teaspoons cornstarch*
> *¼ teaspoon salt*
> *½ teaspoon sugar*
> *¼ teaspoon ground white pepper*
> *2 teaspoons sesame oil*
> *2 teaspoons thin soy sauce*

24 flat-leaf parsley leaves
1 to 2 tablespoons minced cooked lean bacon
1 tablespoon oil
½ pound fresh broccoli or fresh asparagus, cut in large finger-sized pieces

BROTH

> *1 cup chicken broth*
> *¼ teaspoon sugar*
> *¼ teaspoon salt or to taste*

4 teaspoons cornstarch mixed with 2 tablespoons water
Soy-Oil Dip (page 174; optional)

DIRECTIONS FOR COOKING

1. Lightly squeeze off some marinade from mushrooms. Reserve marinade.

2. Grease a heatproof plate with oil. Arrange mushrooms undersides up on plate. Fill each mushroom with about a tablespoon of shrimp mixture. Spoon the remaining shrimp mixture into round balls around mushrooms. Press a piece of parsley on each ball and stuffed mushroom, and top with a little minced bacon. Cover and steam over high heat for 5 minutes. Turn off heat. Cover to keep hot.

3. While steaming the stuffed mushrooms and shrimp balls, heat 3 quarts of water to a rolling boil. Add 1 tablespoon oil. Immerse the broccoli or asparagus in water, and immediately pour it into a colander. Arrange the vegetable on a serving platter with flower tips pointing around edges of platter. Spoon cooked stuffed muchrooms and shrimp balls on top. Cover to keep hot. Reserve juice that is left from the plate.

4. Put broth in a small pot, add remaining marinade and the reserved juice, and bring to a gentle boil. Stir in the cornstarch water. When sauce thickens, pour evenly on stuffed mushrooms and shrimp balls. Serve hot with or without dip.

TEAHOUSE STUFFED PEPPERS WITH
BLACK BEAN SAUCE

Makes 24

PREPARATION OF INGREDIENTS

*12 medium-sized frying peppers or small bell peppers: wash, cut each in
half lengthwise, discard seeds and ribs*
about 2 tablespoons cornstarch

FILLING (mix in a bowl, stir vigorously with a spoon for a minute)

> *1 pound ground pork (containing 10 to 15 percent fat)*
> *⅓ cup minced water chestnuts*
> *4 Chinese dried mushrooms: soak in hot water until spongy, discard
> stems, mince caps*
> *⅓ cup minced scallions, including some green*
> *½ teaspoon sugar*
> *½ teaspoon ground pepper*
> *1 tablespoon cornstarch*
> *2 teaspoons black soy sauce*
> *1 tablespoon thin soy sauce*
> *1 tablespoon sherry*

4 tablespoons oil for pan-frying
1 teaspoon minced fresh ginger
2 teaspoons minced garlic
2 tablespoons salted black beans: rinse in hot water, drain, mash to paste

BROTH MIXTURE (put in a bowl)†

> *1½ cups clear chicken broth (not condensed)*
> *½ teaspoon sugar*
> *2 tablespoons cornstarch*
> *1 tablespoon thin soy sauce*
> *2 tablespoons sherry*

DIRECTIONS FOR COOKING

1. Dust insides of peppers with 2 tablespoons cornstarch.

2. Stuff peppers with filling, pressing it down with a knife.

3. Heat a large skillet over medium heat. Swirl in 4 tablespoons oil. When oil is hot, arrange half the stuffed peppers, meat side down, in skillet. Pan-fry peppers until meat sides are golden brown but are not thoroughly cooked. Drain and let oil drip back to skillet. Transfer peppers to a heatproof plate, meat side up. Put aside for later use. This may be prepared hours or a day in advance.

4. Pan-fry the remaining stuffed peppers in the same manner; put them on another heatproof plate. Keep the oil in skillet for later use.

5. Put one plate of stuffed peppers on a steamer tray. If you have a steamer that has two trays, you may steam both plates of peppers at once by stacking the trays. Cover and steam over high heat for 15 minutes. Turn off heat.

6. While the peppers are being steamed, heat oil that was left in skillet over medium heat. When oil is hot, drop in ginger, garlic, and black beans. Stir constantly. When garlic begins to turn golden, pour in broth mixture. Stir and cook until sauce thickens. Turn off heat. Cover to keep hot. This sauce can be prepared in advance. Reheat in a small pot when it is needed.

7. When stuffed peppers are done, pour sauce over peppers. Serve hot as an appetizer or as a meal with rice.

STEAMED CRESCENTS FILLED WITH CRABMEAT SOUP

Makes about 24

These are the pride of a teahouse chef. The crescents have paper-thin skin, are big as a small coin purse, and are filled with a pocketful of good soup with crabmeat. The secret is that we mix the broth with the gelatinlike agar-agar and gel it. When it becomes solid, we cut it into small squares, combine it with the filling, and stuff it in the crescents.

When the crescents are steamed, the heat turns the gelled agar-agar back into soup. Thus, the crescents are soup-filled.

PREPARATION OF INGREDIENTS

1 cup dried agar-agar (see page 195), loosely packed
2 cups clear chicken broth

FILLING (mix in a bowl, keep refrigerated before use)†

> *1 cup fresh or frozen crabmeat: drain on paper towels*
> *4 ounces fresh shrimp: shell, devein, rinse in running cold water, pat dry, cut into pea-sized pieces*
> *4 ounces lean pork: cut into pea-sized pieces*
> *5 Chinese dried mushrooms: soak in hot water until spongy, discard stems, cut caps into small squares*
> *½ teaspoon salt*
> *¾ teaspoon sugar*
> *⅛ teaspoon ground white pepper*
> *2 tablespoons thin soy sauce*
> *2 teaspoons sesame oil*

WRAPPERS

> *1½ cups all-purpose flour*
> *1 egg: beat to mix yolk and white*
> *cold water*

Ginger-Soy-Vinegar Dip (page 172)

DIRECTIONS FOR COOKING

1. Hours or a day before making crescents, cook agar-agar in chicken broth until it is completely dissolved. Pour in a shallow dish. Cover and refrigerate for a few hours or until it gels. Dice gelled agar-agar into small pieces and mix with the filling; refrigerate before use.†

2. Mix flour and egg. Add water a little at a time until a soft but not sticky dough is formed and knead until dough is smooth and elastic. Roll dough into a long sausage, 1 inch in diameter. Cut dough into walnut-sized pieces and roll them into round balls; cover with a damp towel.

3. Dust working area with a little flour. Roll a piece of dough into a paper-thin circle. Put about a tablespoon of filling in the center of the circle. Fold circle in half to look like a half-moon. Pleat the top curved edge, then pinch the pleated edge and the unpleated edge firmly together to seal the crescent, which now looks like a coin purse (see illustrations on pages 44–45). Gently tap to flatten crescent's round bottom so that it can stand straight. Place crescent between towels. Make the remaining crescents in the same manner.

4. Place a layer of cheesecloth on the bottom of a steamer; arrange crescents on cloth. Cover and steam crescents over high heat for 10 minutes. Serve hot with dip.

Note: Crescents (before steaming) can be made only a few hours in advance; refrigerate until ready to use.

SHAO MAI

(STEAMED PASTRY WITH SHRIMP AND PORK FILLING)

Makes about 48 shao mai

In Chinese, shao mai means "cook to sell," and in fact they are one of the best-selling dim sum in teahouses. For Chinese gourmets, good shao mai should be filled with plenty of shrimp along with pork. However, shrimp is expensive in this country and even more so in the Orient; few teahouses are generous with it, and most simply do not put in any.

For the Chinese, shao mai is usually a breakfast dish. But they make a splendid appetizer or lunch. They are not only delicious but very attractive if served in their bamboo steamer.

Shao mai are easy to make. You can make them in advance, but be sure to keep them refrigerated until steaming, for shrimp goes bad quickly at room temperature. Or you can quickly freeze them uncooked and they will keep for about a week or sometimes two. Steam them while they are still frozen. Of course they taste best when fresh. This recipe is one of three taken directly from *The Classic Chinese Cookbook,* because shao mai is one of the most basic and foremost of dim sum.

PREPARATION OF INGREDIENTS

48 shao mai skins or wonton skins

FILLING (mix well, beat vigorously with a wooden spoon for about a minute, refrigerate until use)†

> *1 pound fresh shrimp: shell, devein, clean with running cold water,*
> *   pat dry, cut into chunks as big as cranberries*
> *1 pound ground pork (containing 10 to 15 percent fat)*
> *⅓ cup Chinese dried mushrooms: soak in hot water until spongy,*
> *   discard stems, mince caps*
> *1 tablespoon cornstarch*
> *1 teaspoon sugar*
> *1 teaspoon salt*
> *¼ teaspoon ground pepper*
> *1 tablespoon sherry*
> *2 tablespoons thin soy sauce*
> *2 tablespoons sesame oil*

Soy-Oil Dip (page 174)

DIRECTIONS FOR COOKING

1. If wonton skins are used, trim skins into circles. Spoon about 1 tablespoon of filling in the middle of a circle; pleat and press skin around filling. The shao mai now looks like a miniature cupcake. Gently squeeze shao mai in the middle crosswise, to narrow its waist. Press down the top to firm up the filling. Lightly tap shao mai to flatten bottom so it can stand up. Make the others in the same manner. Cover and refrigerate them until steaming.

2. Grease a perforated tray or the bottom of a steamer with oil.

Arrange shao mai on it. Cover and steam over boiling water and high heat for 12 minutes (20 minutes if frozen). Serve hot with dip.

Note: *To freeze the uncooked shao mai, do not stack them directly on each other, but separate each layer with wax paper.*

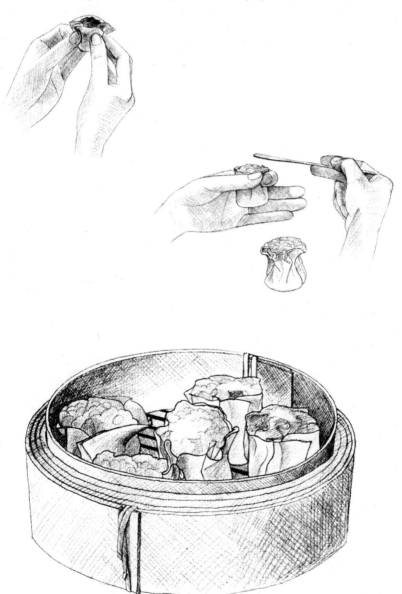

HAH GAU

(STEAMED SHRIMP CRESCENTS)

Makes about 24

No one can resist a hah gau, a savory that pleases all hearts. Many Chinese consider it the most exquisite dim sum. It brings pleasure to every bite. It reflects the art and creativity of Chinese cuisine, transforming a few common ingredients to pure gastronomic delight.

"Hah" means shrimp, and "gau" small crescent. A good hah gau must meet these requirements: the skin should be thin and translucent to show the shrimp wrapped within; the shrimp must be *sonng*—the Chinese standard of well-cooked shrimp, a combination of springiness, crunchiness, and a little resilience felt between one's teeth; the size of the hah gau should be dainty, not larger than a chestnut, to show its maker's skill, for it is much easier to make it larger.

Hah gau skin is made of wheat starch instead of flour. Wheat starch contains no gluten and is therefore inelastic and fragile. This often dismays inexperienced hands. Don't be discouraged if your early efforts do not produce hah gau quite as dainty as you would like. Just keep practicing; be patient and remember the old saying: "Failure is the mother of success."

PREPARATION OF INGREDIENTS

1 cup wheat starch (see page 215), sifted
¾ cup boiling water
1 tablespoon lard

FILLING (mix in a bowl, keep refrigerated until use)†

½ pound fresh shrimp: shell, devein, rinse in running cold water, drain, pat dry, cut into pea-sized pieces
6 water chestnuts, minced

2 tablespoons minced pork fat or bacon fat
½ teaspoon salt
½ teaspoon sugar
2 teaspoons sesame oil
2 teaspoons sherry

Soy-Oil Dip (page 174)

DIRECTIONS FOR COOKING

1. Prepare the hah gau skins: Put wheat starch in a medium-sized bowl, and make a well in the center. Pour in boiling water, stirring quickly with a spoon. Add lard, and knead dough until it is homogenized. Then roll dough into a 1-inch-diameter sausage. Cover with a warm damp towel and let it rest for about 15 minutes. Cut dough into chestnut-sized pieces and roll them into round marbles. Cover them with a towel.

2. Assemble the hah gau: Oil one side of a cleaver or the blade of a broad knife. Press oiled blade on each marble of dough to make a thin circle. Put about 1½ teaspoons of filling in the center of each circle. Make hah gau according to illustrations on pages 44–45.

3. Place hah gau on an oiled steamer basket. Cover and steam over high heat for 10 minutes. Serve hot with dip.

CHA SIU BAU

(STEAMED BARBECUED PORK BUNS)

Makes about 16

Cha siu bau, one of the most famous Cantonese buns, is among the most popular of dim sum. Buns are prepared all over China, but these Cantonese buns are unique because of their soft resiliency. These buns can be resteamed without losing their resilience. This recipe is adapted from *The Classic Chinese Cookbook*.

PREPARATION OF INGREDIENTS

FILLING

> *3 tablespoons lard or shortening for stir-frying*
> *2 teaspoons minced garlic*
> *10 to 12 ounces Chinese Barbecued Pork (page 118): cut into pea-sized pieces*
> *1 tablespoon oyster sauce*
> *1 tablespoon plus 2 teaspoons black soy sauce*
> *2 tablespoons all-purpose flour*
> *1 tablespoon sugar*
> *6 tablespoons water*

BUN DOUGH

Step 1

> *1 teaspoon active dry yeast*
> *¼ cup lukewarm water*
> *½ cup cake flour (not self-rising cake flour) or low-gluten flour, sifted*

Step 2

> *2 cups cake flour, sifted*
> *½ cup very fine sugar*
> *½ cup warm water*

Step 3

> *1 cup cake flour, sifted*
> *2 teaspoons baking powder*
> *1 tablespoon lard*
> *¼ cup slightly warm water*

DIRECTIONS FOR COOKING

To prepare the filling, heat wok over high heat until it is hot. Add 1 tablespoon of the lard or shortening for stir-frying and spread it around. When lard is hot, drop in garlic and stir for a few seconds. Add barbecued pork. Stir-fry for about 15 seconds. Add oyster sauce and 1 tablespoon black soy sauce. Stir and mix well. Remove pork to a bowl.

Keep wok hot over medium heat. Add the remaining 2 tablespoons lard or shortening. When it is hot, add the 2 tablespoons flour and 1 tablespoon sugar. Stir-fry quickly for a few seconds. Swirl in remaining 2 teaspoons black soy sauce and 6 tablespoons water. Mix and stir constantly until it becomes a paste. Return the pork to wok. Mix well. Put in a bowl and cool in refrigerator. (The filling can be prepared hours or a day in advance.)

To prepare the bun dough, use ingredients as specified in steps in the ingredients list:

Step 1: Dissolve yeast in the lukewarm water in a bowl; then add the flour to the yeast water. Mix well. Cover, but do not let the cover touch the dough. Keep in a warm place (an unheated oven) for 15 minutes.

Step 2: In a mixing bowl, thoroughly mix Step 2 ingredients with the yeast dough from Step 1. Cover, but do not let the cover touch the dough. Keep in a warm place for 2 hours or until the dough doubles in size.

Step 3: In a big mixing bowl, thoroughly mix the 1 cup cake flour and 2 teaspoons baking powder; then knead with the dough from Step 2. Gradually add lard and ¼ cup slightly warm water. Mix to form dough. Turn dough out onto a slightly floured surface and knead until homogenized. Put dough in a bowl and cover, but do not allow cover to touch the dough. Keep in a warm place for about 2 hours or until double in size. Press dough down and roll it into a sausage 1½ inches in diameter. Cut sausage into 16 equal sections and roll them into round balls. Cover with a towel to prevent drying.

To assemble the buns, first cut 16 pieces of wax paper, each 1½ inches square. Roll a piece of round dough into a circle about 2½ inches in diameter, but not less than ¼ inch thick. Pinch the outer edges of the circle to make them slightly thinner than the center. Put about a tablespoon of filling in the center of the circle. Pull and gather together the edges, then pinch and twist the pleated edges to seal. Put the flat bottom on a piece of wax paper (to keep the bun from sticking to the steamer or other surfaces), and cover with a towel. Prepare the other buns in the same manner. Allow covered buns to rise for 15 minutes in a warm place before steaming.

Arrange buns, at least ½ inch away from each other, in bamboo steamer basket or on a round rack lined with one layer of cheesecloth. Cover and steam (see steaming methods on pages 184–188) over high heat for 15 minutes. Serve buns hot. (Do not eat the wax paper, of course!)

Notes: *Steamed buns can be frozen; resteam after thawing.*

If you prefer a sweet filling, fill each bun with a heaping tablespoon of sweet red bean paste.

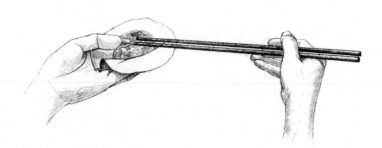

STREET FOOD

**(From the Sidewalk Food Stalls
and Back Lanes)**

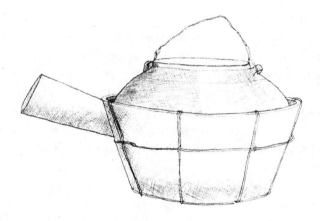

STARLIGHT SHRIMP

Makes 1 pound

There are places called "the poor people's nightclub" throughout the Orient. One is in Kowloon around an old temple, the Queen of Heaven, not far from the harbor. There, a few classmates and I used to while away many evenings when we should have been studying in our college dorm.

It was not a disco or a cabaret, but caravans of food stalls and vendors jamming the back lanes and parking lots at night. In streams of brilliant lights oceans of fun seekers and crowd lingerers slowly flowed.

The sweet aroma of shellfish scented the air. Surging steam from the noodle stalls shot the dark still sky. Roasted ducks with golden skin and spiced innards excited appetites. This was "the poor people's nightclub" in which a poor man ate like a king—a place where gourmets enjoyed the best snake soup and plates of seafood without the dollars draining away. It was also a place to listen to the amateur singers and musicians trying their art. If the sound pleased the crowd, someone would throw in a few coins; if not, some would spit and mutter away.

The height of the evening was about ten, when hungry stomachs and restless spirits were eager to roam the night. We ate from stall to stall, at the small tables with tiny stools, or right off of bamboo skewers as we strolled the streets. With many others we strained our ears as fortunetellers told their humble clients' fate, or watched palmists examining worn and weathered hands. Sometimes we looked for bargains, bought a few things, or just followed the crowd.

If our purses were full, we treated ourselves at the shellfish stalls. Unaware of the stars above and the sweetness of our youth, we savored plates of shrimp, snails, and clams and leisurely watched the crowd pass by.

Many times since then I have returned to this nightclub of the poor. The richness of the night still remained. The same sweet aroma, voices, and salty air greeted the crowd. People still moved unhurriedly as before, except now and then tourists were herded like ducklings hastening by.

PREPARATION OF INGREDIENTS

1 pound fresh medium-sized shrimp within shells: keep in ice water in refrigerator until use

MARINADE

   1 tablespoon sea salt or coarse salt
   1 teaspoon sugar
   1 teaspoon paprika
   1 teaspoon five-fragrance powder
   1 tablespoon fresh ginger juice (use garlic press) or minced ginger
   1 tablespoon sherry

4 tablespoons lard
2 tablespoons peanut oil
¼ cup snipped parsley

DIRECTIONS FOR COOKING

1. Holding shrimp with one hand, with the other hand take a sewing needle and go under the vein crosswise at third section (near the tail), lift the vein, and pull it out gently with the needle. Devein the others in the same manner. Rinse shrimp in very cold water, drain, and pat dry.

2. Combine deveined shrimp and marinade in a bowl, and keep it in refrigerator for an hour before use.

3. Heat wok over high heat. When it is hot, add lard and oil and spread to heat until it begins to smoke. Quickly add shrimp, including its marinade. Stir-fry for about 3 minutes. Drop in the parsley and continue to stir-fry for another 2 minutes or until shrimp turns bright orange and is just cooked. Transfer to a serving platter. Serve hot. Eat with your fingers. Suck and taste the seasoning on the shell before peeling and eating the shrimp.

STEAMED STREET CLAMS

Another great evening enjoyment on the streets is eating piles of clams with a delicious dip made with fresh chili peppers, soy sauce, oil and vinegar. The dip is also good with lobsters and shrimp.

PREPARATION OF INGREDIENTS

Clams for steaming (allow at least a pound per person)
Fresh Chili Pepper-Soy-Vinegar Dip (page 172)

DIRECTIONS FOR COOKING

Scrub clams with a brush and rinse in cold water. Put clams in steamer basket(s) over boiling water. Cover and steam over high heat for about 7 minutes or until clams open. Serve hot with dip.
Note: If shrimp are used, blanch each pound of unshelled fresh shrimp in 4 cups of boiling water with 2 slices of fresh ginger and 2 tablespoons of sherry for 35 seconds. Drain. Serve hot with dip. For larger amounts of shrimp, increase water, ginger, and sherry, but not the cooking time.

BAMBOO STICK CHICKEN

Serves 4 as a meal, 8 as a snack

PREPARATION OF INGREDIENTS

2 tablespoons lard
2 tablespoons oil

SAUCE MIXTURE (mix in a bowl)†

½ teaspoon thyme
2 teaspoons paprika
2 tablespoons sugar
1 tablespoon minced garlic
2 tablespoons black soy sauce
2 tablespoons lemon sauce (page 204)
½ cup plum sauce

2 pounds boned, skinless chicken breasts or thighs: pound gently with the
   sharp edge of a cleaver, cut into 1½-inch squares
½ cup snipped parsley
1 green and 1 red bell pepper: discard seeds and ribs, cut into 1½-inch
   squares

DIRECTIONS FOR COOKING

1. Heat lard and oil in a small pot over low heat. When oil is hot, stir in sauce mixture. Cook, stirring constantly until it bubbles gently. Remove from heat.

2. In a mixing bowl, combine chicken, heated sauce, and parsley; marinate chicken for about 1 hour.

3. Thread chicken pieces and peppers on bamboo or metal skewers and put them on a shallow pan. Brush skewered chicken generously with all the marinade. Grill chicken under broiler for 15 minutes, turning once. Arrange the skewers on a platter and top with the sauce left in the pan. Serve hot with or without rice.

KWANGCHOW BUCKET CHICKEN

Serves 4 as a meal

The people of Kwangtung are renowned for preparing chicken. As you would travel through Kwangtung province by train, at each village stop vendors would rush to the car windows offering pieces of chicken cooked according to the specialty of the village. Weichow, my father's birthplace, is famous for its salt-roasted chicken. My mother and grandmother's village makes the best pure-cut chicken and soy sauce chicken. And Kwangchow, my birthplace, gave birth to this delicious bucket chicken.

It is said that originally a vendor poached the chicken in a large amount of soy sauce, sugar, and many spices, then carried it in shoulder buckets, hawking it on the streets of Kwangchow.

In my region we judge that a perfectly cooked chicken should still be red in the thigh bone. If the thigh bone, the thickest part of the chicken, is thoroughly cooked, then the rest of the chicken is overcooked. But if there is still redness around the thigh, then the meat will be silky and tender.

We also believe a poached chicken is best because without fire underneath the chicken the juice is not drawn out so the chicken retains its natural sweetness. This chicken can be eaten cold and is excellent for picnics.

PREPARATION OF INGREDIENTS

13 cups water
12 ounces rock sugar (or regular sugar)
3 tablespoons salt
4 cups black soy sauce

SPICES (wrapped and tied in cheesecloth)

8 star anise
2 tablespoons flower peppercorns
2 tablespoons cloves
2 cinnamon sticks: break each in half
2 nutmegs
4 ounces fresh ginger root: cut into large chunks

1 fresh chicken, 3½ pounds
1 tablespoon sesame oil

DIRECTIONS FOR COOKING

1. In a large pot combine the water, rock sugar, salt, soy sauce and spices. Cover and simmer over low heat for about an hour. Add chicken, breast side down in sauce. As soon as the sauce liquid comes to a full boil again, cover pot with a tight lid and remove from heat. Poach chicken for 30 minutes. (Do not remove lid while poaching!)

2. Remove chicken from sauce, and brush with sesame oil. Allow chicken to cool before chopping or carving. Chop or carve chicken as desired. Serve hot or at room temperature, with or without rice.

Note: It may seem to you 30 minutes is too short a time for cooking a chicken. But the chicken continues to cook while it is cooling. However, if it is a 4-pound chicken, poach it for 40 minutes. Chickens over 4 pounds are not suitable for this recipe.

You can freeze the leftover sauce, including the bag of spices, and use it again—there should be enough to make two more chickens. (If there is not enough sauce for poaching a whole chicken, use it for cooking chicken wings or livers.)

CHICKEN SHREDS IN MUSTARD SAUCE

Serves 8 as an appetizer

The distant clappings of bamboo sticks and the jingling of bells woke the silence of dawn. The sounds heralded the food vendors. Our breakfast was near.

Like most of the families in China, we often bought our breakfast on the streets. Besides offering great variety, the vendors had their specialties and secret recipes on which their livelihood depended.

The Noodle Man clapped his bamboo sticks six times every time he paused to rest. The sound of bells signaled the Congee Woman, whose young son trotted beside her with a bell. The melancholy cry belonged to Bun Woman Wong; at night her husband hawked cakes and sweet almond soup.

Many a time when we children feared a test we pretended to be sick, but the approaching breakfast never failed to lift us out of our beds. As we gabbed about what we were going to eat, my grandmother's maid loosed her high call at the still silent street, "Buying!," a matinal command she thoroughly enjoyed. Swinging and springing in bouncy strides, the vendors raced to her call. Suspended from the ends of their thick shoulder poles were pots of steaming hot food on flaming stoves, plus sauces, ingredients, and even water for washing bowls.

We would choose from bowls of rice congee with chopped meats; noodles in tasty soup with slices of pork and beef; crispy fried crullers and meaty hot buns. From their portable kitchens they prepared our food, then quietly and proudly presented it to our table. While we savored every bite from our bowls, they patiently waited outside in the morning mist. Having rinsed and dried the bowls we returned them, and the vendors moved on to other doors. Always they padded through streets and lanes, while we students in school studied how things ought to be.

Much has happened on the streets as the generations have progressed. Weddings and births have mended the sorrow of deaths. Old faces have vanished and new voices arise. But the sounds announcing the vendors continue to parade by. The call "Buying!" echoes in the streets much the same as it did in the past.

PREPARATION OF INGREDIENTS

¼ cup uncooked skinless peanuts or walnuts
1 cup oil for frying nuts

CHICKEN MIXTURE (mix in a bowl)†

2 chicken breasts: bone, skin, cut into matchstick strips
1 egg white: beat slightly
4 teaspoons cornstarch

2 cups sliced cucumber or thin celery strips
6 scallions: shred into 1½-inch strips, including some green

SAUCE MIXTURE (mix into a smooth sauce no more than 15 minutes before serving, otherwise mustard will lose its power; cover)

4 teaspoons Colman's mustard powder
4 teaspoons sugar
4 teaspoons water
2 tablespoons Chinese red vinegar
2 tablespoons plus 2 teaspoons black soy sauce
2 tablespoons sesame oil
several strips of red bell pepper or shaved carrot for garnish

DIRECTIONS FOR COOKING

1. Deep-fry peanuts or walnuts in oil until golden brown. Drain on paper towels to cool. Put nuts in a plastic bag and crush them into small pieces with a rolling pin. Put aside.

2. Blanch chicken mixture in water (see Cooking Methods).

3. Arrange cucumber slices or celery strips and half the scallions on a serving platter, then top with the chicken shreds. Pour sauce mixture over chicken evenly and garnish with remaining scallions, crushed nuts, and red pepper or carrot. Serve at room temperature.

BACK LANE WONTON-NOODLE SOUP

Serves 4 to 6 as snack or as a meal

Wonton-noodle soup is one of the most popular and cheapest snacks or meals among the Chinese. There are hundreds of wonton-noodle houses and thousands of street stalls on back lanes and alleys in the Orient.

Good wonton-noodle houses are always small and crowded. The furnishings are seldom more than a dozen bare tables with wooden chairs and stools on a tile floor, and a few hand-written menus pasted on the stark walls.

Nobody minds, or expects more, for we know it is not a place to stretch one's legs, or hold hands with loving eyes. A professor of mine lost all his dates over bowls of wonton-noodle soup. For his ladies lost half their hearts across the still-wet table, and the other half was wiped out by the loud-voiced waiter, who took and called out their orders before they could reach their seats. No love could spring and flow under dozens of hungry eyes measuring the noodles in your bowl, and faces that flashed: Eat and out! I need your table to have my bowl!

Unlike the regular restaurants that cook in their kitchens in the back, the wonton-noodle houses do all the cooking visibly at one side of the entrance.

The delicious scent of freshly cooked noodles and wontons sweeps over you as you step in from the street. At one side stands the cook, enveloped in clouds of hazy steam billowing from huge pots of boiling soup and stock. His hands move with lightning speed, flying among bowls of chopped scallions, oils, sauces, trays of uncooked wontons, fresh noodles, tender broccoli or yu choy (a delicious green vegetable), and stacks of serving bowls.

Usually the menu has less than six items to choose from. Along with the specialty, wontons in soup with or without noodles, small plates of tender vegetables in soy-oil or oyster sauce are the most favored side order to accompany the meal. If one prefers a more meaty snack, small dishes of spiced stewed beef brisket and tasty tender pig's feet are also on the menu to complement the wontons and noodles.

It is not uncommon to wait for twenty minutes to sit down, then share a table with blank-faced strangers. No headwaiter helps you locate a seat. Experienced eyes sweep across the tables searching for a bowl that is nearly empty, then dash to stand guard by its holder, fearful that he or she may order another bowl.

Finally the bowl, surging with an irresistible aroma, is delivered to the table. The world becomes a void of sweet contentment, consisting only of the luscious wontons and noodles.

No one would dare to linger at the table when the last drop of soup is drained. As you are barely emerging from the sphere of sheer gratification, the waiter mops under your nose, calling out from the bottom of his lungs to the cashier guarding the door, "Come four dollars and one week," meaning four dollars plus seven dimes (in Hong Kong money). The satisfied creature pays according to the call, retaining every cent of change, willing to leave the alluring scent—temporarily.

PREPARATION OF INGREDIENTS

8 ounces fresh egg noodles
45 to 50 wonton skins: cover to keep from drying

FILLING (mix in a bowl, refrigerate before use)†

½ pound pork (better with 10 percent fat): ask your butcher to grind it once only, or grind it in food processor
½ pound shrimp: shell, devein, rinse in running cold water, pat dry, cut into peanut-sized pieces
¼ teaspoon salt
¼ teaspoon sugar
⅛ teaspoon ground pepper
2 teaspoons pale dry sherry
2 teaspoons sesame oil
1 tablespoon thin soy sauce
1 beaten egg
2 scallions: cut into pea-sized pieces, including some green

1 large pot of water (about 14 cups)

continued

BROTH MIXTURE (mix in a 3-quart pot)†

    6 cups clear chicken broth (not condensed)
    ¼ teaspoon sugar
    salt to taste

½ cup scallions in pea-sized pieces, including some green
1 tablespoon sesame oil (optional)
½ pound fresh broccoli, cut into finger-sized pieces, or 1 bunch of
    watercress
Soy-Oil Dip (page 174)
a dish of Chinese chili sauce (or Tabasco sauce)

DIRECTIONS FOR COOKING

1. Cook egg noodles as for Cold Plain Noodles (page 143). Put noodles in a large serving bowl. Set aside.

2. Prepare a small bowl of water for sealing wontons. Take a wonton skin and keep the rest covered. Put about 1 heaping teaspoon of filling in the middle of a wonton skin. Moisten edges with water and fold skin in half; press edges together and seal tightly; bring the folded corners over each other and seal with water. Put wonton between linen towels. Prepare the others in the same manner.

3. Bring the large pot of water to a rapid boil, and at the same time simmer the broth mixture over very low heat.

4. Drop wontons in boiling water and cook over moderate heat for about 5 minutes; remove wontons with a Chinese drainer or a large slotted spoon and place them on top of the cooked noodles in the serving bowl. (Save water for cooking the vegetable.)

5. Pour broth over wontons and noodles, and add scallions and sesame oil (if you wish).

6. Bring water back to a rapid boil. Immerse broccoli or watercress in water; remove it right away with a Chinese drainer and add it to the wonton-noodle soup.

7. Serve each person a bowl of wonton-noodle soup with vegetables, a small dish of dip, and sauce. Eat wontons and noodles with dip or sauce, adding it to the spoon, but try not to mix sauce or dip with soup; otherwise you have peppery soy sauce soup.

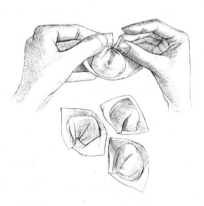

CLASSIC SHRIMP WONTON SOUP

Serves 4 as a meal

PREPARATION OF INGREDIENTS

*1 pound fresh shrimp: shell, devein, wash in cold water, drain, cut into
pea-sized pieces*
1 tablespoon salt
4 cups water

MARINADE (combine in the order given, refrigerate)†

¾ teaspoon salt
1 teaspoon cornstarch
¼ teaspoon sugar
⅛ teaspoon ground white pepper
1 teaspoon sherry
½ egg, beaten
2 tablespoons minced bamboo shoots
2 tablespoons minced scallions, white part only

45 wonton skins: cover to keep from drying
1 large pot of water (about 5 quarts)

BROTH MIXTURE (mix in a 3-quart pot)†

5 cups clear chicken broth (not condensed)
¼ teaspoon sugar
salt to taste

¼ cup scallions in pea-sized pieces, including some green
1 tablespoon sesame oil
1 pound yu choy or broccoli: wash and cut into finger-sized pieces

SAUCE MIXTURE (mix in a small pot)†

2 tablespoons lard or oil
¼ cup oyster sauce
1 tablespoon sherry
1 tablespoon sesame oil

Soy-Oil Dip (page 174)
a dish of Chinese chili sauce or Tabasco sauce

DIRECTIONS FOR COOKING

1. In a mixing bowl, combine shelled shrimp, salt, and 4 cups water; rub the shrimp in your hands for about a minute, and put in refrigerator for about 30 minutes.

2. Rinse shrimp thoroughly in running cold water for a few minutes; pour in a colander, drain, and pat dry with towels.

3. In a mixing bowl, combine shrimp and marinade, and stir to mix well. Refrigerate until use.†

4. Prepare a small bowl of water for sealing wontons. Take a wonton skin and keep the rest covered. Put about 1 heaping teaspoon of the marinated shrimp in the middle of a wonton skin. Moisten edges with water and fold skin in half; press edges together and seal tightly; bring the folded corners over each other and seal with water. Put wonton between kitchen towels. Prepare the others in the same manner.

5. Bring the large pot of water to a rapid boil, and at the same time simmer the broth mixture over very low heat.

6. Drop wontons in boiling water and cook over moderate heat for about 1 minute; remove wontons with a Chinese drainer or a large slotted spoon to a large serving bowl. (Save water for cooking the vegetable.) Add broth, scallions, and sesame oil to wontons; cover to keep hot.

7. Heat sauce mixture over low heat until it bubbles. Remove from heat and cover to keep hot.

8. Bring water back to a rapid boil. Immerse yu choy or broccoli in water, and allow it to stay in for about 15 seconds. Remove vegetable with a Chinese drainer to a serving platter and drain off water from vegetable. Discard water from pot. Pour heated sauce over vegetable and serve as a side dish with the wonton soup.

9. Give each person a small dish of dip, sauce, and a bowl of wonton soup. Dip wonton in dip or sauce, but try not to mix sauce with the soup itself; otherwise you have soy sauce soup.

DINNER IN A CLAY POT

(CHINESE SAUSAGES AND VEGETABLE COOKED IN A CLAY POT)

Serves 2 to 4 as a meal

We children knew our pig had gone when sausages and bacon tied in large bundles were suspended from big iron hooks. If the harvest was good, sweet potatoes were piled high in a corner below the sausages and bacon; brown cane sugar bars were stacked neatly in black glazed barrows—but it was the rice in huge baskets that took up most of the cellar's floor.

"This will last us through winter," grandmother would whisper to her maid, Noble Face, her voice low and guarded so that no jealous spirits could hear and do evil to our staple food. But the quick tilt at the corners of their mouths and their unworried eyes revealed that a fat year was here.

In Chinese villages, curing sausages and bacon was strictly a fall affair, for they needed to be air-dried in the crisp autumn air. Chinese houses had neither refrigerators nor central heat, but the sausages and bacon stayed unspoiled throughout the fall and winter months.

Not every Chinese could afford to have sausage or bacon on the dinner table. For the poor, it was a luxury; for the rich, a simple pleasure. Also, it was a Chinese New Year gift from subordinates to their bosses.

This dish is offered in many restaurants and food stalls during the chilly months. You can order a small pot, enjoying it in pleasing solitude, or share a larger pot with one who shares your heart. The piping hot pot bearing the sweet smell of earth, and the steaming scents of sausages and rice, raises not only the appetite but also the feeling of loving, warmth, and home.

PREPARATION OF INGREDIENTS

*1 ½ cups long-grain rice: wash and rinse several times in cold water until
  water is not cloudy, drain*
2 cups cold water
2 Chinese pork sausages: rinse in cold water, pat dry
2 Chinese duck-liver sausages: rinse in cold water, pat dry
*4 ounces Chinese Barbecued Pork (page 118) or Smithfield ham
  (optional)*

SAUCE MIXTURE (mix in a bowl)†

> *3 tablespoons black soy sauce*
> *3 tablespoons water*
> *¾ teaspoon sugar*

6 ounces yu choy or fresh broccoli: wash, cut into finger-sized pieces

DIRECTIONS FOR COOKING

1. Put drained rice and water in 3-quart Chinese clay pot (see
page 188). Spread rice evenly. Cook over medium heat until rice
comes to a full boil, and continue to cook for 2 minutes. Place both
kinds of sausages and barbecued pork or ham on top of rice. Put
lid on. Turn heat to low, and cook for 10 minutes. Then turn off
heat, but do not remove pot from burner and *DO NOT PEEK!*
Allow pot to stay covered for another 15 minutes.

2. When the rice is almost done, put sauce mixture in a small
saucepan, stir, and cook over medium-low heat until it comes to a
gentle boil. Turn off heat. Cover to keep hot.

3. Just before serving, bring 2 quarts of water mixed with 1
tablespoon oil to a rapid boil. Add yu choy or broccoli and turn off
heat at once. Let vegetable stay in pot while you are preparing the
following steps.

4. Remove sausages and pork or ham from rice. Cut them
diagonally into thin slices. Return them, with slices overlapping
each other, on top of rice at one side of the pot. Drain the
vegetable, and arrange it on the other side. Pour sauce over
sausages, vegetable, and pork or ham evenly.

5. Bring pot and its contents to the table and serve hot at once.

MINCED BEEF WITH BLACK BEAN SAUCE ON RICE

Serves 4 to 6 as a meal

PREPARATION OF INGREDIENTS

3 tablespoons oil

SEASONINGS (put in a bowl)†

> *1 tablespoon black beans: rinse in hot water, drain, mash into paste*
> *2 teaspoons minced garlic*
> *2 scallions: cut into pea-sized pieces, including some green*

1 pound lean beef: mince by hand or grind in food processor (do not grind into paste)

SAUCE MIXTURE (mix in a bowl)†

> *½ teaspoon salt*
> *½ teaspoon sugar*
> *4 teaspoons cornstarch*
> *2 tablespoons black soy sauce*
> *¼ cup pale dry sherry*
> *1 cup clear chicken broth (not condensed)*

½ cup green peas
¼ cup coarsely chopped red bell pepper
3 eggs: beat to mix yolks and whites
4 to 6 cups hot Plain Rice (page 103)

DIRECTIONS FOR COOKING

1. Heat wok over medium heat. Swirl in the oil. When oil is hot, drop in the seasonings. Stir-fry until garlic turns golden; add beef. Stir and cook beef until it is no longer red. Stir in sauce mixture; stir and cook until sauce begins to bubble. Add peas and red bell pepper. Mix well. Swirl in beaten eggs. Do not stir until eggs begin to set around the edges. Stir and mix until sauce thickens. Turn off heat.

2. Put rice on a large serving platter and top with the beef mixture. Serve hot.

SPICY BEEF SNACK

This delicious beef finger snack is regarded quite highly among Chinese. It is usually packed in gift boxes and sold in Chinese food shops as a present. Because it is light, dried, nourishing, and can be kept for weeks without refrigeration, it is a wonderful treat for camping, hiking, or a trip.

PREPARATION OF INGREDIENTS

3 pounds beef roast (rump roast): cut into ⅛-inch-thin slices

MARINADE (mix in a bowl)†

2 tablespoons sugar
¼ teaspoon cayenne pepper (ground red pepper)
1 teaspoon curry powder
½ cup plus 1 tablespoon black soy sauce
1 tablespoon Chinese Shaohsing rice wine or sake

GLAZE (mix in a bowl)†

2 tablespoons plus 2 teaspoons honey
2 tablespoons water
1 tablespoon thin soy sauce

DIRECTIONS FOR COOKING

1. In a mixing bowl, dip beef slices in marinade to coat evenly.
2. Lay beef slices on large trays to dry overnight in a cool place or in refrigerator, turning from time to time.
3. Preheat oven to 250 degrees.
4. Lay beef slices on wire racks on cookie sheets or baking pans lined with foil. Bake in oven for 30 minutes or until beef is stiff and dry. Remove from oven.
5. For a sweeter beef, brush beef with glaze while still hot; or you may prefer it without the glaze.
6. Store beef slices in plastic bag. They can be kept in refrigerator for weeks; also they keep well for days without refrigeration.

SPICED COLD BEEF, CHINESE MOSLEM STYLE

Serves 8 as an appetizer

A small minority of Chinese are Moslems, whose restaurants specialize in beef and lamb dishes. This delicious cold spiced beef dish was a re-creation of an old memory that haunted my family periodically. In my youth, we occasionally visited a small Chinese Moslem restaurant near the Pearl River Bridge of Canton, where thousands of restaurants, markets, food stalls, and vendors densely flocked.

Years later, the restaurant could no longer be found. The spiced beef haunted us more often. We then tried out a few Moslem restaurants in Hong Kong, but their beef did not offer the same flavor that our tastes could recognize.

In order to quench our pressing yearning, we Leungs created our own version of this Moslem dish several years ago in Hong Kong. After many suggestions, arguments, and preparations, we finally agreed that this was the dish—or at least very close to it—of our memory. What we could not put into it were the gaiety of those noisy streets near the Pearl River Bridge, the cozy little Moslem restaurant, and our youth.

PREPARATION OF INGREDIENTS

1 cup oil
¼ cup uncooked skinless peanuts
4 ounces ground beef (use hamburger)
2 tablespoons Szechwan sweet bean sauce or ground bean sauce

SAUCE MIXTURE (mix in a bowl)†

   ½ teaspoon cayenne pepper
   ½ teaspoon flower peppercorn powder
   3 tablespoons sugar
   1 tablespoon minced garlic

3 tablespoons white vinegar
3 tablespoons black soy sauce
1 tablespoon sesame oil

8 bay leaves
1 flank steak or 1½ pounds tender beef: trim off fat
1 cup celery in thin strips, 1½ inches long
½ cup scallions in thin strips, 1½ inches long
¼ cup red bell pepper in strips and a handful of watercress

DIRECTIONS FOR COOKING

1. Heat 1 cup oil in wok to deep-fry temperature. Deep-fry peanuts over medium-low heat until golden brown. Remove peanuts with a slotted spoon or a drainer. Drain on paper towel to cool. Put peanuts in a small plastic bag or between towels, then roll and crush them coarsely with a rolling pin. Put aside for later use.

2. Remove all but 2 tablespoons oil from wok. Heat oil. When oil is hot, add ground beef. Stir and cook until it is done. Add bean sauce, and mix with beef. Stir in sauce mixture and mix well. Turn off heat. This meat sauce can be prepared a few hours in advance.

3. Fill a big pot with water (enough to cover the flank steak or beef). Bring water and bay leaves to a rapid boil. Add meat, cover, and cook over medium heat for about 10 minutes or until the meat is medium rare or done to your taste. Remove meat from water and pat dry. Put meat on cutting board and slice it into thin pieces as you would slice roast beef. Arrange slices, slightly overlapping each other, on a serving platter. Garnish with celery strips, scallions, red pepper and watercress.

4. Pour meat sauce over beef slices evenly, and sprinkle crushed peanuts on top. Serve at room temperature. Plain Cold Noodles (page 143) are a good accompaniment.

MAI LEUNG'S COILED MEAT BREAD

Makes two rounds, each 1 inch thick and 8 inches in diameter

Crusty outside, meaty and tasty inside, this kind of hot bread is very popular in the northern and eastern parts of China, where people eat bread, biscuits and noodles more than rice. It is made at home as well as sold at street stores or in back lane shops.

After years of experimenting with various kinds of bread from different regions, I have combined the best elements into this delicious coiled meat bread.

It is easy to prepare and loved by old and young. You may serve it with soup as a meal and it is also marvelous for picnics.

PREPARATION OF INGREDIENTS

FILLING (mix in a bowl):

> ½ teaspoon salt
> ½ cup minced Smithfield ham or sandwich ham or cooked bacon
> 2 teaspoons five-fragrance powder
> ½ cup minced scallions, including some green

DOUGH

> 2 cups all-purpose flour
> 1 ¼ teaspoons salt
> 1 teaspoon sugar
> 2 tablespoons baking powder
> ¾ cup cold water

1 tablespoon sesame oil
4 tablespoons sesame seeds
oil for pan-frying
2 teaspoons honey mixed with 1 tablespoon water

DIRECTIONS FOR COOKING

1. In a mixing bowl, combine flour, salt, sugar and baking powder with your hands. Add water gradually and knead with your hands until dough is smooth. (The dough should be soft and a little sticky.) Cut dough into two equal portions and roll each into a ball.

2. Divide filling into two equal portions.

3. Dust working area with flour. With a rolling pin, roll each ball into a large pancake about 10 inches in diameter; brush each pancake generously with sesame oil to within ½ inch of the rim and sprinkle each evenly with a portion of filling. Then roll each pancake into a sausage as you would roll up a jelly roll. Pinch ends

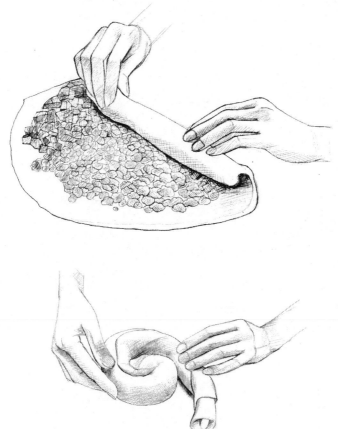

to seal in filling. Coil each sausage to make a round cake. With a rolling pin, roll each coiled cake into a large round, about 7 inches in diameter. Brush the top of each round with a little water, then sprinkle each with sesame seeds. Press seeds in dough with hand or with a rolling pin.

4. In a large heavy skillet, add enough oil to reach about halfway up the dough. Heat oil over low heat. When oil is hot, add one of the dough rounds, seeded-side up; cover and fry over *low heat* until golden brown on one side, then turn and fry until done, about 7 minutes in all. Transfer to a chopping board and brush the seeded side with honey water. Cut bread into wedges. Serve hot or at room temperature.

Note: *If you want a sweet bread, use the filling in the recipe for Fried Sweet Sesame Balls (page 126).*

KUO-TIEHS, PEKING STYLE

(SOFT AND CRUSTY CRESCENTS)

Makes 24 crescents

Kuo-tiehs roughly means "sticking to skillet." These crescents are steamed meaty and juicy chaiotses pan-fried until golden brown and crusty on the bottom, but still soft and moist on the upper sides. Kuo-tiehs are one of the most beloved snacks and informal meals in many parts of China.

PREPARATION OF INGREDIENTS

Steamed Chaiotses, Peking Style (page 40)
about ½ cup peanut or vegetable oil
Ginger-Soy-Vinegar Dip (page 172) and a small dish of Chili Oil (page 170)

DIRECTIONS FOR COOKING

1. Prepare and steam chaiotses according to recipe.
2. Pour about ¼ cup oil in each of two medium or large heavy skillets (oil should be deep enough to cover skillet bottom generously). Heat oil over medium heat, and when it is hot, add half the chaiotses, wide bottom down, on each skillet. Cover and pan-fry them over medium-low heat until they are golden brown and crusty on the bottom. Remove with a spatula to a serving platter, crusty side up. Serve hot with dips at once.

Note: If kuo-tiehs stick to the skillet, it is because they have not been fried long enough to become really crusty. So be patient. When they are ready, they can be lifted easily with a spatula.

SZECHWAN SPICY CUCUMBERS

Serves 8 or more as an appetizer

PREPARATION OF INGREDIENTS

*4 firm cucumbers (about 3 pounds): wash, cut each in half lengthwise,
  scoop out and discard seeds and soft part, cut into strips 1 by 3 inches*
2 tablespoons salt
1 tablespoon sugar
1 cup red bell peppers in thin strips
2 tablespoons thinly shredded fresh ginger root
2 tablespoons oil
2 tablespoons sesame oil
4 dried chili peppers: break each in half (use seeds too)
1 teaspoon flower peppercorns

SAUCE MIXTURE (mix in a bowl)†

   ¼ cup Chenkong (sometimes romanized as Chen-Chiang) vinegar
   ¼ cup sugar
   1 tablespoon black soy sauce

DIRECTIONS FOR COOKING

1. Combine cucumbers with salt and sugar; allow to stand at room temperature for 15 minutes. Rinse cucumbers thoroughly in a large bowl under running cold water; drain in a colander; pat dry. In a large bowl, combine cucumbers with bell peppers and ginger shreds.

2. Heat two kinds of oil in a small pot over low heat. Gently fry chili peppers and flower peppercorns to golden brown, then cool slightly. Add sauce mixture, and pour over cucumber mixture. Stir and toss to mix well. Refrigerate for a few hours or more. Serve as an appetizer or as a side dish.

Note: Keep the remaining vegetables in a covered jar with sauce; they will keep for 3 or 4 days.

BEEF CONGEE WITH CONDIMENTS

Serves 6 as a meal or as a snack

The Chinese call congee "jook." It is rice cooked in plenty of water. After hours of cooking, it becomes a thin smooth gruel; then various kinds of meat or seafood are added at the end of cooking. In the Orient, congee is a very popular breakfast, which was on the table every morning during our recent visit throughout ten cities of China. Also, it serves as a late evening snack at home, at street stalls, or in small sidewalk restaurants. And it is an excellent lunch or an informal meal.

PREPARATION OF INGREDIENTS

¾ cup rice: soak in water for 2 hours or more, drain before cooking
2 teaspoons salt
1 tablespoon oil
4 cups oil for deep-frying
½ cup uncooked skinless peanuts
1 ounce bean thread noodles or rice sticks
20 wonton skins: cut into ¼-inch-wide strips
1 pound lean beef: ask your butcher to grind it once, or grind it in the food processor
1 tablespoon thin soy sauce
½ teaspoon sugar
1 tablespoon sesame oil
½ cup chopped scallions, including some green
⅓ cup chopped fresh coriander leaves (optional)

DIRECTIONS FOR COOKING

1. In a large pot, bring 12 cups of water to a rapid boil. Add soaked rice, salt, and 1 tablespoon oil. Uncover, and cook over medium heat for about 2 hours or until rice becomes like thin gruel. There should be at least 8 cups congee left in pot at the end

of cooking time. Add boiling water to maintain the 8-cup level if it is necessary. (You may prepare congee hours in advance; and reheat over low heat on stove.) Simmer congee over very low heat to keep hot.

2. While the congee is cooking, heat oil to deep-fry temperature (375 degrees). Deep-fry peanuts until golden brown. Drain, cool, and put in a small serving bowl.†

3. Reheat oil to deep-fry temperature. Loosen noodles or rice sticks by pulling them apart. Test oil by dropping in a piece of noodle or rice stick; if it pops up and turns white instantly, the oil is right. Deep-fry noodles; they will pop up and turn into a white nest instantly; quickly turn over the nest and fry the other side. (This takes less than 10 seconds.) Drain on paper towels, then crumble them by hand. Set aside.

4. Separate wonton strips, then deep-fry half at a time until they are golden brown. Drain on paper towels. Put on a serving plate.†

5. In a mixing bowl, combine ground beef, fried bean thread noodles or rice sticks, soy sauce, sugar, and sesame oil until they are thoroughly mixed.

6. Add beef mixture to the simmering congee. Stir to mix well. Cook until beef is no longer red. Turn off heat.

7. Serve congee hot in individual bowls. Bring peanuts, fried wonton strips, scallions, and coriander to the table. Let each person add condiments to his or her congee.

CHICKEN AND ABALONE CONGEE

Serves 4 to 6 as a meal

PREPARATION OF INGREDIENTS

¾ cup rice: soak in water at least 4 hours, drain before using
½ teaspoon salt
1 tablespoon oil

CHICKEN MIXTURE (mix in a bowl, refrigerate before use)†

> *2 chicken breasts: bone, remove skin and trim off fat, pound chicken*
> *with the back edge of a cleaver, cut into ½-inch cubes*
> *1 teaspoon minced fresh ginger root*
> *1 tablespoon cornstarch*
> *¼ teaspoon white pepper*
> *¼ teaspoon sugar*
> *1 tablespoon sesame oil*
> *1½ tablespoons thin soy sauce*
> *2 teaspoons sherry*

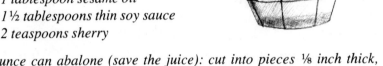

16-ounce can abalone (save the juice): cut into pieces ⅛ inch thick, ½
inch wide, and 1½ inches long

CONDIMENTS

> *¼ cup chopped fresh coriander leaves (in a small serving bowl)*
> *½ cup chopped scallions, including some green (in a small serving*
> *bowl)*
> *¼ cup sesame oil (in a small serving bowl)*
> *¼ cup thin soy sauce (in a small serving bowl)*
> *½ cup skinless uncooked peanuts: deep-fry in 1 cup oil until golden*
> *brown, drain, put in a serving bowl*

DIRECTIONS FOR COOKING

1. Bring 12 cups of water to a rapid boil. Add soaked rice, salt, 1 tablespoon oil, and the juice from the abalone. Uncover and cook over medium heat for about 2 hours or until rice becomes like thin gruel. There should be 8 cups congee left in pot at the end of cooking time. Add boiling water to maintain the 8-cup level if necessary.†

2. Keep congee bubbling over medium heat. Add chicken mixture. Stir to separate pieces. As soon as the chicken is cooked (about 45 seconds), add abalone. Turn off heat. Stir to mix well.

3. Bring the condiments to the table. Serve congee hot in individual serving bowls. Let each person add the condiments to his or her congee.

DEEP-FRIED GHOSTS

(CHINESE CRULLERS)

Makes about 26

I have not invented this name. These most popular breakfast crullers have always been called deep-fried ghosts since the time before my great-grandparents and theirs. The story of these crullers was passed down to every child. It is one of those stories that every Chinese loves to tell.

During the Sung Dynasty, the Kingdom of Chin often invaded Sung. And Yueh Fei (1103–1141), a patriot of Sung endowed with unusual strength, vowed to serve his country and people. His mother tattooed on his back four Chinese characters: Tsin Chung Pao Kuo, meaning "With unfailing loyalty to the country." And he devoted his life entirely to the military and became a general.

Repeatedly, he defeated the invader's army, and he was greatly loved and revered by the people of Sung. When he was at the apex of his triumph, a high official named Ch'in Kuai persuaded the king to issue twelve edicts, commanding Yueh Fei to withdraw his troops and return to the capital. Obedient, he was jailed, tortured, and charged with high treason; and he was poisoned to death in jail.

The people of Sung loved Yueh Fei as profoundly as they hated Ch'in Kuai, and the hatred also extended to Ch'in Kuai's wife. In a fury, the people stuck two pieces of thin dough together, symbolizing Ch'in Kuai and his wife, and deep-fried them in hot oil to express their helpless rage. In Chinese, the word "Kuai" sounds like the word for "ghosts." And these crullers are called Deep-Fried Ghosts as well as Deep-Fried Kuai.

These crullers are the secret, the livelihood, and the pride of small back-lane restaurants and sidewalk stall vendors.

Making them is not as simple as it might seem. This recipe was developed from hours of work and practice with two chefs in Hong Kong.

PREPARATION OF INGREDIENTS

2 teaspoons alum (obtain in a drugstore)
⅓ cup hot water
1 cup cold water
2½ teaspoons salt
1 tablespoon baking soda
1 teaspoon baking ammonia (obtain in a drugstore)
8 ounces cake flour (not self-rising cake flour)
8 ounces high-gluten (high-protein) flour
oil for deep-frying

DIRECTIONS FOR COOKING

1. In a large mixing bowl, stir alum constantly in ⅓ cup hot water until it dissolves; if there is a small undissolved amount left, discard it. Add the cold water, salt, baking soda, and baking ammonia; mix well. Stir in flour and toss to mix gently with both hands. (Do not knead!) When a dough is roughly formed, put it on a floured surface and work in the following manner:

2. Press dough down gently with your fists. Fold dough and press with fists again. Repeat this process a few times. Cover dough with a damp cloth or a plastic bag to rest for about 15 minutes. Then repeat pressing, folding, and resting three times. Cover dough with a damp cloth and let it rest at room temperature for 7 to 12 hours (7 hours in hot weather, 12 in cold weather) before use.

3. When ready to begin, put it on a floured surface. With a rolling pin gently roll dough into a rectangular sheet ½ inch thick and 4 inches wide.

4. Place about 4 inches oil in a large (preferably 16-inch) wok and heat to deep-fry temperature over medium heat.

5. Dust a cleaver blade with flour. Cut dough sheet crosswise into strips ¾ inch wide by 4 inches long. Discard end pieces. With a cleaver gently lift up a strip and place directly on another strip. Use the dull edge of the cleaver (be sure it is floured) to press lengthwise (not all the way through) down the middle of the stacked strips. Gently pick up both ends of the stacked strips and

stretch to about 12 to 14 inches long. Immediately put in hot oil, turning it constantly with chopsticks. Deep-fry until cruller turns golden brown and has expanded about three times its original size. Drain on paper towels. You may deep-fry three or four crullers at a time. Serve hot or at room temperature. The Chinese custom is to serve crullers with congee (page 95).

Note: Crullers can be frozen in plastic bags. Reheat uncovered on a tray in a 350-degree oven for about 7 minutes or until crisp.

CRUNCHY JELLYFISH SKIN IN SOY-VINEGAR-OIL

Serves 4 as appetizer

This dish is for gourmets only, not for those who squeal at anything unfamiliar. However, most of our American friends have had jellyfish skin in our house without knowing it. For after it is prepared and cut into strips, it becomes "those crunchy things."

Like most treasured delicacies of the Chinese, such as shark fin and sea slug, jellyfish skin has very little taste of its own. It has to borrow flavors from other ingredients.

The Chinese enjoy it tossed with red vinegar, soy, and sesame oil as an appetizer or as a snack. We also use it to add texture to salad, cold noodle dishes, or congee.

PREPARATION OF INGREDIENTS

½ pound dried jellyfish skin: rinse off salt, soak in plenty of cold water for at least 4 hours, rinse thoroughly before use
1 small cucumber: peel, cut in half lengthwise, scoop out seeds, cut crosswise into thin slices
½ teaspoon salt
¼ cup scallions cut into thin strips, including some green
several thin strips of red bell pepper or shaved carrot for garnish

DRESSING (mix in a bowl)†

½ teaspoon sugar
¼ teaspoon salt
1 tablespoon red vinegar
2 teaspoons thin soy sauce
2 teaspoons sesame oil

DIRECTIONS FOR COOKING

1. Bring a large pot of water to a boil. Immerse soaked jellyfish skin in water, then quickly remove it from pot and rinse in cold running water. (By now it has shrunk to half of its size.) Pat dry. Cut into thin strips. Set aside.

2. Mix sliced cucumber and salt in a bowl; allow it to stand for 30 minutes. Rinse in cold water. Drain and pat dry.

3. Put cucumber slices on a serving plate and top with the jellyfish skin. Sprinkle with scallions and red pepper or carrot. (This may be prepared hours in advance, and refrigerated until used.) Add dressing just before serving. Toss at the table. Serve cold or at room temperature.

STREET-STALL BEEF TRIPE

Makes about 4 cups

PREPARATION OF INGREDIENTS

10 cups water
8 bay leaves
2 pounds frozen honeycomb tripe: thaw, rinse thoroughly
in running cold water
2 tablespoons peanut or vegetable oil
2 teaspoons fresh minced ginger

SAUCE MIXTURE (mix in a bowl)†

4 star anise
1 tablespoon sugar
3 tablespoons black soy sauce
2 tablespoons Szechwan chili bean sauce
1 teaspoon ground bean sauce
½ cup Chinese Shaohsing wine or pale dry sherry
¼ cup beef or chicken broth

a small dish of Chinese chili sauce or Tabasco sauce (optional)

DIRECTIONS FOR COOKING

1. Put water and bay leaves in a large pot, bring to a boil, and add tripe. When water again comes to a rapid boil, put lid on and turn off heat. Allow tripe to stay covered in hot water for 2 hours. (Do not peek or disturb the tripe during this time; the heat in the water will cook it to the right doneness.) Discard water and bay leaves. Cut tripe into pieces 1½ inches long and ½ inch wide. Put in colander and shake it to drain off excess water. Pat dry; keep in refrigerator until use.

2. Heat oil in a Chinese clay pot or a 3-quart pot over low heat

for several seconds. When oil is hot, drop in ginger; stir and cook until it is golden. Pour in sauce mixture, stir, and cook for a few minutes. Add tripe and mix with the sauce. Cover and simmer for about 5 minutes. Remove from heat. Let tripe soak in sauce for a few hours or overnight. Just before serving, heat tripe in sauce over low heat until it is hot. Serve hot with or without chili sauce or Tabasco.

PLAIN RICE

Makes about 6 cups

PREPARATION OF INGREDIENTS

2 cups long-grain rice: wash and rinse several times in cold water until water is not cloudy; drain
3 cups cold water

DIRECTIONS FOR COOKING

1. Use a 3-quart pot with a tight lid. Put in the washed rice and add the water. Cook over medium heat without a cover. When it is boiling, you will see that the water is very foamy, almost obscuring the rice. Do not go away! Stand by and watch it closely. You will see the water evaporating to the point where many small holes (like craters) appear in the rice. The Chinese call them "rice eyes."

2. Put lid on, turn heat to very low, and cook for 10 minutes. Then turn off heat, but do not remove the pot or uncover it. Let it stay covered for 15 minutes or more. (Do not peek during this 25 minutes—the magic steam will escape, and you will have half-cooked rice for not having faith!)

3. Remove the cover. Loosen the rice with a fork or a chopstick. Serve hot. (If it is to be used for fried rice recipes, cool in refrigerator overnight.)

PLAIN RICE

(USING RICE COOKER)

Wash and rinse 2 cups long-grain rice in cold water until water is not cloudy. The washing will reduce the starch in the rice, eliminating its stickiness, and give a shining coat to the rice.

Drain rice and follow the instructions that come with the cooker. The best part of a rice cooker is that it also keeps rice hot for at least an hour or more.

COOKING GLUTINOUS RICE

Glutinous rice is a much richer and stickier rice than other kinds of white rice. It needs less water and easily sticks to the bottom of the pot while cooking. The best way to cook glutinous rice is to soak it thoroughly, then steam it, and it always comes out perfectly.

Wash and rinse glutinous rice with cold water until water is not cloudy. Cover the rice with plenty of cold water and soak for at least 6 hours or overnight at room temperature, or till rice is plump and breaks easily if pressed with fingernail.

Drain rice in colander. Line a steamer basket with a layer of cheesecloth and steam (see steaming methods, page 184) for 20 minutes or until rice is cooked.

FESTIVAL FOOD
AND TEAHOUSE SWEETS

CHINESE NEW YEAR SAVORY
TURNIP PUDDING

Makes one 9- by 1 ½-inch pudding

Before every Chinese New Year, one of the holiday foods that many families busily prepared was this pudding. Everybody made plenty, and my grandmother made more than everybody else, so that it would not be exhausted during the holiday. It sat on every cupboard, on shelves, tables, bookcases, on empty bunk beds, and a few even were secluded in my bureau. My mother frowned and quietly objected.

Whoever came through our doors, if they ever wished to come back again, had to eat great quantities of my grandmother's turnip pudding—along with tea and sweets—even though they might already have a stomachful from the Wangs', the Chans', and the Lees' tables.

Besides prizing herself as the best turnip pudding maker in the neighborhood, Grandmother also had a gift for commanding others to eat, not by physical force, but by sheer eye power, staring food into others' throats.

After experiencing the agony of a nearly bursting stomach, relatives and friends learned to stop at the Leungs' first before visiting the other households. When the pudding finally vanished from the territories occupied, my grandmother had again proved to my mother that her pudding was not only delicious but was barely enough to supply the demand. Her happiness was complete, and so was mine when the last pan of turnip pudding was gone from my bureau.

This sumptuous pudding is for those who love the flavor and aroma of turnips. Turnips have a strong smell while cooking. If people are not acquainted with it, they might think there is a mild sewage problem.

So share it with those who love it, as a meal, lunch, or tea snack.

PREPARATION OF INGREDIENTS

2 teaspoons lard or shortening
½ strip Chinese bacon: discard skin, cut into pea-sized pieces
3 Chinese pork sausages: cut into pea-sized pieces
6 large Chinese dried mushrooms: soak in hot water until spongy, discard stems, cut caps in small pieces
⅓ cup Chinese dried shrimp: soak in hot water to soften, cut into small pieces
1½ to 2 pounds Chinese white turnip: peel, grate by hand or shred in food processor
½ cup water
½ cup clear chicken broth (not condensed)
1½ cups rice powder
¼ teaspoon ground white pepper
1½ teaspoons salt
1 teaspoon sugar
1 tablespoon thin soy sauce
2 tablespoons white sesame seeds: roast in an ungreased pot over low heat until golden brown
a small bowl of Chinese chili sauce or Tabasco sauce

DIRECTIONS FOR COOKING

1. Heat wok over medium heat until it is hot. Add lard or shortening. When it is hot, drop in bacon and sausages; stir-fry until they sizzle. Add mushrooms and shrimp; stir-fry for about 30 seconds. Turn off heat, and put mixture in a bowl. Do not wash the wok.

2. Add grated turnip and ½ cup water to wok, cook over low heat until turnip becomes soft, then turn off heat. Return sausages, bacon, mushrooms, and shrimp mixture to wok; add the remaining ingredients except the sesame seeds and chili or Tabasco sauce. Mix well.

3. Grease a 9-inch cake pan with vegetable oil, and pour in the

pudding mixture. Spread and smooth it out with a spoon. Sprinkle sesame seeds on top.

4. Steam pudding mixture over boiling water for about 1 hour or until the tip of a knife comes out clean. Allow to cool for about 5 minutes. Serve hot with Chinese chili sauce or Tabasco sauce.

Note: Turnip pudding can be prepared in advance and resteamed. Also, you may slice cold pudding into squares and pan-fry them with a little oil until crisp and golden brown outside but still soft inside.

FESTIVE COUNTRY CRESCENTS

Makes about 20

The skin of these country crescents is slightly crisp outside, deliciously soft and glutinous inside. They are a favorite traditional food, made only during the fall and winter when harvest is finished.

On my family's land, there was much to be done before making these crescents: the grains were harvested by the hired hands, then husked in a seesaw-shaped stone grinder driven by their feet. While we children looked for field mice, the bond maids—who were really slaves, but also beloved and authoritative members of the family—dug and busheled the turnips, taros, and yams. Trays of river shrimp, trapped by our uncles, were dried in the sun, and so were beans of red, black, green, and yellow color; Grandmother sorted and stored them in clay jars. Since we had no marshland to grow water chestnuts, we traded a basket of our yams for them with our neighbor called Deaf Man.

We also bought from him each year a barrel of delicious fat rice worms to be salted and spiced and eaten as a treat throughout the winter months. When the green vegetables and melons were picked, the maids pickled the mustard greens, blanched the bok choy, and hung them on bamboo poles to dry. Then we all watched and cheered the men chasing the squealing pigs, yelling our advice on how to squeeze them into the sausagelike pig baskets, and feeling slightly sorry when they were carried away. They were shouldered back as pork to be barbecued and made into sausages, ham, and bacon. This was done by the women in the house, commanded by Grandmother's boisterous voice. Grandmother loved commotion, running feet, active hands; even the children were called in to string the sausages and hang the bacon.

When the labor was over, the cold-storage bin full, a silent contentment prevailed over both old and young. To boast of our prosperity would tempt the dark and jealous spirits, who were always as near as the blessings of the gods.

In quiet happiness, then, we prepared these crescents to celebrate the first day of winter and again the Lunar New Year. To give thanks for the harvest, the benefits of the old year and the promise of the new, we offered them to the gods and the spirits of our ancestors. We exchanged them with friends and relatives to wish each other good harvest and good luck. We also took care to have plenty for ourselves to feast on all day long.

PREPARATION OF INGREDIENTS

2 tablespoons oil

FILLING (group them on a plate)†

> *1 tablespoon dried shrimp: soften in hot water 15 minutes, mince*
> *5 Chinese dried mushrooms: soak in hot water until spongy, discard stems, mince caps*
> *about ½ pound Chinese Barbecued Pork (page 118): cut into pea-sized pieces (to make 1 cup)*
> *⅓ cup bamboo shoots cut in rice-sized pieces*
> *⅓ cup water chestnuts cut in rice-sized pieces*

SAUCE MIXTURE (mix in a bowl)†

> *2 teaspoons thin soy sauce*
> *¼ teaspoon salt*
> *¼ teaspoon sugar*
> *¼ teaspoon five-fragrance powder*

WRAPPERS

2 cups unsifted glutinous rice powder
¾ cup plus 2 tablespoons boiling water
2 tablespoons lard or shortening
2 ½ tablespoons sugar

oil for deep-frying

DIRECTIONS FOR COOKING

1. Heat wok hot over high heat. Add 2 tablespoons oil. When oil is hot, add shrimp, mushrooms, and pork; stir-fry for about 10 seconds. Drop in bamboo shoots and water chestnuts. Stir in sauce mixture and cook for about 15 seconds. Put on plate, cover, and cool in refrigerator.†

2. Sift rice powder in a mixing bowl; add boiling water and stir quickly. Knead into a ball. Add lard or shortening and sugar and knead until smooth. Cover with a towel and allow to rest for 10 minutes.

3. Roll dough into 1-inch-diameter sausage. Cut into 20 equal sections. Cover with a towel. Roll each section into a round ball. Grease blade of cleaver (or use a broad-blade knife) with oil. Press blade on ball to make a thin circle, and fill it with 1 tablespoon filling. Fold circle into half. Pinch edges tightly together. Crimp edges. (See illustration.) Put crescents between towels. Make the others in the same manner.

4. Heat oil in wok to deep-fry temperature (375 degrees). Deep-fry crescents, a few at a time, turning them often, until they

are golden (they do not turn brown). Drain on paper towels. Serve hot or warm.

Note: The crescents can be made a day or two in advance before they are deep-fried. Keep in refrigerator until use.

HAPPY FAMILY DUMPLING SOUP

Serves 4 as a meal

These marble-sized smooth, soft, glutinous dumplings signified more than just a snack or meal in our life. They were a symbol of family happiness.

The smoothness and roundness of the dumplings represented a family, full and whole without rough edges; the stickiness symbolized the inseparability and unbreakableness of a family.

Prior to every Chinese New Year, we would assemble around the table, rolling plenty of these glutinous dumplings, taking care to say only things that were cheery and sweet. And the first thing that touched our tongues on New Year's Day was these dumplings in sugared soup, so that we as a family would be sweet and whole in the year to come.

During the Chinese New Year holidays we did nothing but chat and eat. To reinforce our wishes we made more dumpling soup, now with meat and vegetables.

As we gathered and enjoyed the dumplings leisurely, my grandmother's eyes would beam on us, and I knew a wish had been fulfilled.

PREPARATION OF INGREDIENTS

2 tablespoons oil

EGG MIXTURE (beat together until slightly foamy)

> *3 eggs*
> *¼ teaspoon salt*

1½ cups glutinous rice powder
2 teaspoons sugar
about ½ cup cold water

BROTH (mix in a 3-quart pot)†

> *4 cups clear chicken broth (not condensed)*
> *½ teaspoon sugar*
> *½ teaspoon salt (or to taste)*

1 cup Chinese Barbecued Pork (page 118) or Smithfield ham or cooked sandwich ham cut in small squares
10 Chinese dried mushrooms: soak in hot water until spongy, discard stems, cut caps into small squares
2 tablespoons Chinese dried shrimp: soak in hot water until softened, cut into small pieces
2 well-packed cups Chinese celery cabbage in thin strips
2 scallions: cut into pea-sized pieces, including some green

DIRECTIONS FOR COOKING

1. Heat wok hot over medium heat and swirl in the oil. When oil is hot, pour in egg mixture. Slowly swirl mixture by turning the wok clockwise to form a large pancake. Turn pancake over when it is no longer runny; when it is set, transfer to a cutting board; cut into thin strips; put aside.

2. Combine rice powder and sugar in a mixing bowl, add water gradually, and mix with hand to form a smooth dough. Divide dough into three portions. Roll them into ½-inch sausages; then pinch the "sausages" into cherry-sized pieces. Put a small piece in the center of your palms and roll it into a marble-sized dumpling. Repeat the others in the same manner; put dumplings between towels.

3. Add pork or ham, mushrooms, and shrimp to broth and bring it to a rolling boil. Add celery cabbage and cook until broth comes to a rolling boil. Add dumplings and cook over medium heat. As soon as all the dumplings float to the top, turn off heat. Add scallions and egg strips. Serve hot.

FRIED RICE FESTIVAL

Serves 6 as a meal

PREPARATION OF INGREDIENTS

5 tablespoons oil
4 eggs; beat with ¼ teaspoon salt until yolks and whites are mixed
1 cup chopped scallions in pea-sized pieces, including some green
2 Chinese pork sausages: cut into pea-sized pieces
10 Chinese dried mushrooms: soak in hot water until spongy, discard stems, cut caps into ¼-inch squares
¼ pound Chinese Barbecued Pork (page 118) or Smithfield ham or sandwich ham: cut into ¼-inch cubes

SHRIMP MIXTURE (mix in a bowl, refrigerate until use)†

> *½ pound fresh shrimp: shell, devein, rinse in running cold water, pat dry, cut into peanut-sized pieces*
> *1 teaspoon cornstarch*
> *1 teaspoon pale dry sherry*

5 cups cold cooked long-grain rice: cook a day in advance, break up lumps before using

SAUCE MIXTURE (mix in a bowl)†

> *¾ teaspoon salt*
> *½ teaspoon sugar*
> *¼ teaspoon ground white pepper*
> *2 tablespoons thin soy sauce*
> *1 tablespoon black soy sauce*

1 cup fresh or frozen green peas: if they are fresh, blanch in water
1 cup uncooked skinless peanuts (optional): deep-fry in about 2 cups of oil until golden brown, drain on paper towel, put in a serving bowl

DIRECTIONS FOR COOKING

1. Heat wok over medium heat. Swirl in 2 tablespoons oil. When oil is hot, pour egg mixture into wok. Spread eggs by turning and rotating wok. Cook eggs as you would cook a very soft and moist

omelet. Remove eggs from wok to a plate and cut into small chunks for later use.

2. Reheat wok over high heat. Add the remaining 3 tablespoons oil. When oil is hot, drop in ½ cup scallions and sausages. Stir-fry until sausages sizzle. Add mushrooms and barbecued pork or ham; stir-fry for about 30 seconds. Add shrimp mixture; stir-fry about 10 seconds, until shrimp is about half-done. Add rice, and stir in sauce mixture. Add peas and stir to mix well. Return egg chunks to wok. Stir-fry rice mixture, fast and constantly, over medium heat until rice is thoroughly heated. It takes about 10 minutes. Drop in the remaining scallions. Mix well; salt to taste. Serve hot with or without fried peanuts.

Note: Fried rice can be reheated in an ungreased wok over medium heat until it is hot.

LOTUS LEAF RICE

Serves 4 to 6 as a meal

The lotus is a sacred flower of the Orient. It resembles the water lily, but it does not belong to the same family: the lotus grows in muddy ponds, but unlike the water lily, which floats on water, the lotus stands many feet above the water. Therefore, in China, the lotus symbolizes purity, for it grows in mud without being soiled.

Once in an old temple I viewed two ponds of ethereal lotus. The monks guarded them as if they were crown jewels, keeping them behind two locked iron gates and high spiked walls. There, in the man-made concrete ponds, high and majestic they stood, regal on their towering long stems. Some blossoms seemed as large as goddess heads, with luminous wide petals and tinted pink tips. Such an enthralling sight was like watching dawn on a mountain thousands of feet high. It is an awesome beauty.

In the subtropical parts of the Orient, lotus ponds among rice fields are a common scene. Every part of the lotus is usable: the seeds and roots are eaten as fruit or as vegetable, the gently fragrant leaves are used to wrap and give flavor to food, and the flowers grace altar tables in homes and in temples.

In the summer when the lotus was in glorious bloom, people would go to the teahouses and restaurants that had lotus ponds. When the weather was good, tables and seats were clustered about the flower ponds. If the seeds and roots were young, they appeared on the menu. One would munch on the juicy marble-sized seeds and nibble slices of gently sweet crisp roots while revering the splendid sacred lotus.

The high point of the meal was the summer specialty, rice with assorted meats wrapped in fresh lotus leaves tied with straw. Bearing the streaming hot lotus package, the waiter also brought a pair of scissors. Then eyes and breath were seized by the scissors snipping a circle at the top of the leaves. When the circle was lifted, unveiling the fragrant treasures hidden within, spoons and chopsticks dived into the festive rice. Amid scented air, wriggling babies, unsettling children, soft and loud conversations, and bustling waiters, our hearts lightened, and troubles glided away with the summer clouds.

Before the summer ended, farmers would gather the lotus leaves and dry them under the sun, so that teahouses, restaurants and housewives could have rice in lotus leaves in other seasons.

The delicately smoky dried leaves do not flavor the rice as much as fresh ones, but they never fail to bring the festive summer to a Chinese heart.

PREPARATION OF INGREDIENTS

1 pound glutinous rice: soak in plenty of cold water for 5 hours or until it is plump
4 tablespoons lard or oil

CHICKEN MIXTURE (mix in a bowl, refrigerate until use)†

 1 cup boned, skinned chicken in ½-inch cubes
 ½ egg white
 ¼ teaspoon salt
 ¼ teaspoon sugar

⅛ *teaspoon ground white pepper*
1 teaspoon cornstarch
2 teaspoons sesame oil

10 Chinese dried mushrooms: soak in hot water until spongy, discard stems, cut caps into ⅓-inch squares
½ *cup lean pork cut in peanut-sized pieces*

SHRIMP MIXTURE (mix in a bowl, keep refrigerated until use)†

> ½ *pound fresh shrimp: shell, devein, rinse in cold water, pat dry, cut into peanut-sized pieces*
> ½ *egg white, beaten*
> *2 teaspoons cornstarch*
> ¼ *teaspoon salt*
> *1 teaspoon sherry*

SAUCE MIXTURE (mix in a bowl)†

> ½ *teaspoon salt*
> ¼ *teaspoon sugar*
> *1 tablespoon mushroom soy or black soy sauce*
> *2 tablespoons oyster sauce*
> *1 tablespoon sesame oil*

2 large fresh or dried lotus leaves (or 24 dried bamboo leaves if lotus leaves are not available): soak dried lotus or bamboo leaves in warm water until soft; pat dry

DIRECTIONS FOR COOKING

1. Steam soaked rice for 15 minutes or until done (see page 104).

2. Heat wok hot over high heat. Add 3 tablespoons lard or oil. When it is hot, add chicken mixture. Stir-fry about half a minute, until chicken is almost done. Remove from wok.

3. Turn heat to high. Add the remaining tablespoon of lard or oil to wok; drop in mushrooms; stir and cook for several seconds. Add pork; stir-fry until it is no longer pink. Add shrimp mixture; stir and cook until shrimp turns whitish and is almost

cooked. Stir in sauce mixture. Mix well, then turn off heat.

4. Remove half the meat and shrimp mixture from wok to a bowl, and leave the other half in wok. Add cooked rice to wok and mix well with the meat and shrimp mixture.

5. Spread out one lotus leaf. Transfer the rice mixture to leaf, and top with the other half of meat and shrimp mixture. Put the other leaf on top. Wrap as you would wrap a round package. Tie it with straw or string. You may refrigerate the package until steaming. (If bamboo leaves are used, arrange leaves overlapping on a piece of heavy foil about 18 inches square. Transfer rice mixture to the center, then top with remaining meat and shrimp mixture. Place more leaves on top. Gather and fold the corners of the foil together to cover any opening.)

6. Steam the package over high heat for 30 minutes. Using scissors, cut the leaf from top at the table. Serve hot. (Do not eat the leaves, please!)

Note: You may divide the rice mixture into six equal portions. Wrap each portion in a lotus leaf, tie with string, and steam for about 15 minutes. Cut strings before serving. But let your family and guests have the pleasure of opening them.

CHA SIU

(CHINESE BARBECUED PORK)

This barbecued pork is not only eaten as a snack, appetizer, or a meal, but also it is required constantly as an ingredient in Chinese recipes.

Since it is used for so many purposes, and it freezes so well, and cooking it messes up the oven, you might as well make plenty when you make it.

PREPARATION OF INGREDIENTS

about 5 pounds boneless pork loin (tenderloin): cut into strips 2 inches thick and 2 inches wide

MARINADE (mix in a bowl)†

> *6 tablespoons sugar*
> *1 teaspoon salt*
> *4 teaspoons five-fragrance powder*
> *½ cup plus 2 tablespoons black soy sauce*
> *2 tablespoons ground bean sauce*
> *⅔ cup hoisin sauce*
> *½ cup Chinese Shaohsing wine or sake*
> *1 tablespoon minced garlic*

GLAZE (mix in a bowl)†

> *4 tablespoons honey*
> *1 tablespoon thin soy sauce*
> *1 tablespoon sesame oil*

DIRECTIONS FOR COOKING

1. Place pork strips in a large bowl or pan, and put marinade over to coat evenly; put in refrigerator; turn pork from time to time. Allow pork to sit in marinade for at least 8 hours or more.

2. Preheat oven to 500 degrees.

3. Spear pork strips lengthwise with skewers and put them directly on oven rack. (If it is a gas oven, put rack in middle of oven. If electric, put rack in upper part of oven.) Put a big roasting pan with ½ inch of cold water on bottom of gas oven, on lowest rack of electric oven, to catch the drippings and prevent them from smoking. Roast pork for 15 minutes. Turn skewers. Turn oven to 450 degrees. Roast pork for another 15 minutes or until done.

4. Generously brush pork strips with glaze, catching the drippings with a plate. Return pork strips to oven (do not go away) and roast for 1 minute. Turn off heat.

5. Remove barbecued pork from skewers. Cut into thin slices. Brush slices with the remaining glaze if there is any, or the drippings you caught while brushing. Serve hot, warm, or cold.

Note: If you want to freeze pork strips, do not slice them; just freeze the large chunks.

FAMILY WINTER CHICKEN

Serves 8 as a meal

This large dish is a splendid dinner, especially on a wintry day after skiing or shoveling snow. It is delicious, hearty, and nourishing; and it requires very little preparation. You may serve it straight from the pot and eat it in front of a burning fire.

PREPARATION OF INGREDIENTS

4½ to 5½ pounds whole chicken: rinse chicken, gizzard, liver, and heart; remove fat from cavity; cut gizzard and liver into bite-sized pieces; put liver aside
choose four of the following ingredients, ¼ cup of each: dried lotus seeds, barley, red beans, yellow or green split beans, black-eyed peas or lima beans: mix in a bowl, wash thoroughly
10 shelled chestnuts, dried or fresh
4 Chinese dried red dates (optional): slit each with a knife
8 to 10 Chinese dried mushrooms: wash, discard stems
½ cup canned button mushrooms: rinse and drain
1 chunk fresh ginger, as big as a plum: crush it with a cleaver
4 bay leaves
2 teaspoons thyme
1 teaspoon sugar
1 teaspoon ground pepper
2 cups clear chicken broth (not condensed)
¼ cup dry sherry
salt to taste
Soy-Oil Dip (page 174)

DIRECTIONS FOR COOKING

Put chicken (breast side up), heart, and gizzard in a 5-quart Chinese clay pot or metal pot. Add all the other ingredients except chicken liver, salt and soy-oil dip. Pour in enough water to cover 90 percent of the chicken. Bring liquid to a rapid boil. Turn heat to low; cover and simmer chicken for about 2½ hours or until chicken is very tender. (Add water to maintain the water level while cooking if necessary.) Add liver about 10 minutes before the

cooking is done. Skim off fat; salt to taste. Serve hot in individual bowls. Give each person a small dish of dip; use dip sparingly.
Note: Leftovers can be reheated over low heat with a little water.

JONG: DRAGON BOAT FESTIVAL PACKET

(RICE AND MEAT WRAPPED IN BAMBOO LEAVES)

Makes 8 packets

The Dragon Boat Festival honors Chu Yuan, a poetic genius and virtuous statesman who lived about 250 years before Christ.

Chu Yuan was an aristocrat of Ch'u, one of the seven Warring States into which China was divided at that time. While still in his twenties, he was entrusted with a high post. But his youthful brilliance and his counsel to the king of resistance to Ch'in, the most powerful of the Warring States, aroused his rival courtiers to slander his integrity. Thus Chu Yuan was banished. In exile, he wandered about in the South, lamenting in his supremely beautiful poems.

When Ch'in eventually took over Chu Yuan's country and captured the king, Chu Yuan drowned himself in River Mi-lo. Boats raced out to search for his body, and thus originated the Dragon Boat Festival. Worrying about the poet without food, people wrapped rice with meat or sweets in bamboo leaves and cast them into the river to him. And it is this rice packet which the Chinese call *jong*.

For more than two thousand years, every year on the fifth day of the fifth month of the Chinese lunar year, long sleek boats resembling fierce dragons to drive away evil spirits still earnestly race. The boats are never privately owned but belong to villages and towns. The competitive spirit runs extremely high, especially when the villages or towns are traditional foes. In each boat, a drummer directs the oarsmen, whose oars must follow the rhythm of the drum. The boats speed like flying dragons, fluttering banners, racing not only for the honor of Chu Yuan but also for the pride of their village or town and the pleasure of the huge cheering crowd.

And on that day, families continue to wrap plenty of rice in bamboo leaves. The jong has become more and more elaborate through the years. Some varieties are sweetened with bean paste; others flavored with large pieces of meat, egg yolk, mushrooms, chestnuts, and beans. And people no longer send jong down into the river to Chu Yuan but feast on it themselves. Even the faithful ones take packages of jong to a waterfront, burn incense, give many bows to the poet's spirit, but never leave him a *jong*.

This jong is heavy, sticky and musty. The Chinese love it, but not every Westerner takes to it. It will keep at least for a week if it is not opened. It is excellent to take along on a camping trip or a sailing excursion as lunch, snack, or a meal in itself. It should be reboiled before serving.

PREPARATION OF INGREDIENTS

about 3 dozen dried bamboo leaves: wash in warm water, and soak for about 45 minutes; keep leaves in water during wrapping preparation
1 pound glutinous rice: cover with plenty of water and soak overnight; drain in colander; put in a bowl and mix with 2 teaspoons salt, 1 teaspoon sugar, and 2 tablespoons oil
½ pound split skinless mung beans: wash, cover with plenty of water, soak overnight; drain in colander; put in a bowl, and mix with 1 teaspoon salt and 1 teaspoon sugar
½ pound boneless pork belly with skin: cut into 16 pieces; mix with 2 teaspoons salt, 2 teaspoons five-fragrance powder, and marinate overnight
8 salted duck eggs: discard whites, put yolks in a bowl
8 large Chinese dried mushrooms: soak in hot water until just spongy, discard stems
8 shelled fresh or dried chestnuts: if dried chestnuts are used, soak in water for about 1 hour
a small bowl of sugar

DIRECTIONS FOR COOKING

1. Put two bamboo leaves overlapping each other; turn the ends toward you to make a shape looking like a scoop. Put about 2 tablespoons of rice in the dipper, then spread with 1 tablespoon of mung beans. Top with 2 pieces of pork, 1 yolk, 1 mushroom, and 1 chestnut. Add two more leaves, overlapping each other, around

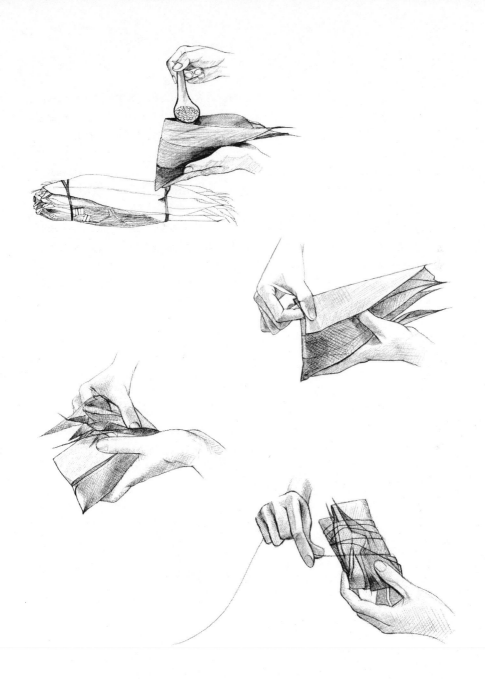

the dipper to build up the wall so that it will hold more. Then spoon 2 tablespoons mung beans and 3 tablespoons rice to cover the previous ingredients. Fold leaves and tie tightly with string or heavy crochet yarn as illustrated. Prepare the others in the same manner.

2. Cover rice packets (jong) with water in a large pot and

simmer over low heat for 6 hours. Remove jong; drain and discard water. Cut string with scissors; discard bamboo leaves; cut jong into slices. Use sugar as dip. Serve hot or at room temperature.

3. To reheat jong: Simmer the unopened one(s) in water for about 20 minutes. But steam the unwrapped leftovers for about 10 minutes (see steaming methods, pages 184–188).

Note: If you want a sweet variety, use only soaked glutinous rice and sweet bean paste. Fill each packet with 3 tablespoons of rice, 2 heaping tablespoons of sweet bean paste, then another 3 tablespoons of rice. The packets are smaller and only need 4 hours of simmering. Use sugar or syrup as dip.

SMILING DATES

Makes about 30

In this recipe, each round of dough is slit before it is deep-fried; when it is cooked, the slit on this round sesame ball resembles a smile—and thus the Chinese call it "smiling date." The pastry is sweet, crisp, and full of sesame. The "dates" are like cookies which can be made in advance and stored in a jar.

Be sure to follow the directions exactly, handling the dough very gently. If you handle it too much, it will release its gluten, which prevents the pastry from expanding in the oil.

PREPARATION OF INGREDIENTS

¼ cup hot water
¾ cup sugar
1 tablespoon baking powder
1 tablespoon oil
1 small egg: beat well
12 ounces cake flour: sift
about ½ cup white sesame seeds
oil for deep-frying

DIRECTIONS FOR COOKING

1. In a mixing bowl, stir hot water and sugar together until sugar dissolves. Cool. Then add baking powder, oil and egg, and beat to mix well with a whisk. Stir in flour and work in the following manner: Do not knead! Use both hands to toss the flour and the liquid together. With your fists press the loose dough lightly, fold dough gently, and press it lightly again.

2. Place dough on a floured surface. Fold dough very gently and press it lightly several times (do not overdo it) until dough is smooth. Put in a plastic bag to rest at room temperature for 1 hour before frying. It can also be kept in the refrigerator for a day before use.

3. Press dough gently into 1-inch-thick rectangle. Dust a Chinese cleaver with flour and cut dough into 1-inch squares. Roll squares into round balls. Wet your hands with water and moisten each ball by rolling between your hands. Roll moist balls in sesame seeds to coat generously. Wash and dry hands. Again roll balls in your hands to allow the sesame seeds to stay on firmly. Put on a tray.

4. Dust the cleaver with flour. With its dull edge, cut a slit into each ball at the center.

5. Pour about 2 to 3 inches oil in wok, and heat over low-medium heat. When oil is about lukewarm, put sesame seed balls, cut side down, on a large Chinese drainer or a large slotted spoon and immerse it in the oil. Remove drainer or slotted spoon. When sesame seed balls begin to float, deep-fry over low-medium heat until they expand to twice their size and turn golden brown. Drain on paper towels. Cool; serve at room temperature. Keep like cookies in a tight container. If they lose their crispness, reheat them in a 350-degree oven until they are crisp.

FRIED SWEET SESAME BALLS

Makes 12 balls

This recipe for sesame-seed balls was taught to me by my grandmother's maid, Noble Face, when my husband and I visited her in her village home in China in the spring of 1979.

Unlike the sesame-seed balls in bakeries in Chinatowns and Hong Kong, and the ones I learned to make from dim sum chefs in Hong Kong, these will stay soft and fresh for a few days instead of becoming hard and unpalatable in a matter of hours.

PREPARATION OF INGREDIENTS

2 cups glutinous rice powder
6 tablespoons plus ½ cup water
½ cup sugar

FILLING (mix in a bowl)†

> *¼ cup sweetened flaked coconut*
> *¼ cup sugar*
> *¼ cup white sesame seeds: roast in an ungreased pot over medium heat, stirring constantly, until golden brown; cool and crush with a rolling pin or grind coarsely in a spice or meat grinder*

ALTERNATE FILLING

> *12 tablespoons sweet red bean paste: roll into 12 balls*

about ½ cup white sesame seeds for coating: put on a plate
oil for deep-frying

DIRECTIONS FOR COOKING

1. Mix ½ cup rice powder with 6 tablespoons of cold water into a thin batter in a mixing bowl.

2. In a pot, stir sugar in ½ cup water until it dissolves; bring it to

a boil. Add batter and stir quickly for several seconds over low heat until batter is clear and thickened. Remove from heat.

3. Combine 1½ cups rice powder with the hot batter and stir. When the dough is not too hot to touch, put it on a slightly powdered surface. Knead until soft and not sticky. If the dough seems dry, wet your hands with water and knead to soften dough. Divide dough into 12 equal sections and roll each into a round ball between your palms. Cover them with a damp cloth.

4. Take a dough ball and make a hollow in the center. Fill hollow with a heaping teaspoon of filling or a bean-paste ball. Close the opening by squeezing edges together with your thumb and your forefinger. Pinch edges to seal and smooth out pinch mark.

5. Wet your hands with water and roll balls in your hands to moisten them. Roll wet dough balls in sesame seeds to coat generously. Wash and dry hands. Roll balls again in hands to make sesame seeds stay firmly on dough.

6. Pour oil in wok to reach about 3 inches deep. Heat oil over medium-high heat. When oil is moderately hot, put sesame seed balls on a large Chinese drainer or a large slotted spoon and put in oil. Allow sesame seed balls to stay on the drainer until they begin to float. Remove drainer. With a spatula, press each ball firmly against the wok. (This pressing action enables the sesame seed balls to expand.) Turn heat to medium-low, so that sesame seed balls will not turn brown too quickly, but allow the dough to cook thoroughly. Roll balls in a circling motion with the bottom of the drainer. And again press balls with spatula. Roll and fry balls until they are golden brown. Drain on paper towels. Cool for a few minutes before serving.

COCONUT ANISE RICE CAKE

Serves 6 to 8

PREPARATION OF INGREDIENTS

*1 pound glutinous rice: soak in plenty of water for at least 4 hours or
    more, drain*
½ cup sweetened flaked coconut
1 to 2 tablespoons anise seed
⅔ cup sugar
3 tablespoons lard or butter

DIRECTIONS FOR COOKING

1. Cook soaked glutinous rice as in Plain Rice (page 103). (Do
not use recipe for Glutinous Rice; it will not be sticky enough for
this dish.)

2. While the cooked rice is still hot, stir in coconut, anise seed,
sugar, and lard or butter. Mix well.

3. Brush an 8- to 8½-inch baking dish with vegetable oil. Pour in
rice mixture, press, and spread it evenly. When it is cool, cut into
squares. Serve at room temperature as a snack.

SUGARY OLD MEN

(SUGAR EGG PUFFS)

Makes about 20

These sweet, airy puffs are favorites among the countless
breakfast and snack items in China. In the morning as we children
walked to school, they were hawked on the streets. Round and
golden, frosted with glittering white sugar, they often loosened
the lunch money lodged in our fists.

In Chinese, the name of this sweet actually means "sugary old
men"; however, no one I have asked could tell me the origin of
this name. It might be that the white sugar on the puffs was seen
as the white hair of an old man.

These sugary old men can be made hours in advance. Be sure to follow the instructions carefully, frying them in warm oil in the beginning. They are excellent for dessert or as a tea snack.

PREPARATION OF INGREDIENTS

1 cup plus 2 tablespoons water
2 tablespoons lard or butter
1 cup all-purpose flour
½ teaspoon baking ammonia (obtain in drugstore)
5 large eggs
oil for deep-frying
about 1 cup sugar

DIRECTIONS FOR COOKING

1. In a medium-sized pot, place water and lard or butter and bring to a rolling boil. Turn off heat. Immediately stir in flour and baking ammonia. Add eggs, one at a time, stirring constantly until batter is thick but smooth. Set aside.

2. Heat oil over low heat. When oil is a little hotter than lukewarm, drop in about 2 tablespoons of batter for each puff. Deep-fry puffs slowly, a few at a time, turning from time to time, until puffs expand four times their original size. This process is usually slow. When puffs reach their maximum size, turn heat to a higher temperature, about medium or medium-high. Deep-fry egg puffs until they turn a rich golden color or a pale brown, and are firm and crisp outside. Drain on paper towels, and roll in sugar to coat evenly while they are still warm.

3. Cool oil to low temperature before putting in batter for another batch of egg puffs; repeat, cooking the remaining egg puffs in the same manner. Serve warm or at room temperature. They can be cooked a few hours in advance, then covered with paper napkins.

Note: If egg puffs do not expand as much as they should, or are still battery inside, turn heat down to very low. Egg puffs expand in low temperature—not instantly, but slowly—so be patient. Also, be sure to raise the oil temperature after egg puffs finish expanding, so that they are firm and crisp outside.

CHINESE NEW YEAR SWEET SESAME BOWS

Makes about 3 dozen

Chinese children love these traditional cookies made to look like bows. Every family, prior to Chinese New Year, makes plenty of them to exchange with relatives, friends, and neighbors. If you need to double the recipe, make it twice, so that you don't have to handle a large dough.

PREPARATION OF INGREDIENTS

2 cups all-purpose flour
6 tablespoons sugar
3 ½ tablespoons lard or butter
½ teaspoon vanilla extract (optional)
1 egg
about ¼ cup cold water
2 tablespoons white sesame seeds
about 3 cups oil for deep-frying

DIRECTIONS FOR COOKING

1. In a mixing bowl, place flour, sugar, lard, and vanilla extract. Rub them together with your fingers. Add egg. Knead to mix well. Add water, a little at a time, until dough is soft but not sticky.

2. Put sesame seeds on a plate. Roll dough in the sesame seeds until it is generously covered.

3. Turn dough onto a floured surface. With a rolling pin, roll dough into a ⅛-inch-thin long sheet. Cut the sheet into 3-by-1-inch strips. Then make a 1-inch slit lengthwise in the middle of each strip. Pick up one end of a strip and put the other end through the slit, and then pull it straight. It looks like a bow.

4. Heat oil in wok over high heat to deep-fry temperature (375 degrees). Deep-fry bows, several at a time, until golden brown. Drain and cool on paper towels. Put in a covered container to preserve crispness.

SWEET WATER CHESTNUT PUDDING

Serves 6

PREPARATION OF INGREDIENTS

1 cup peeled fresh or canned water chestnuts: mince coarsely
½ cup water
1 cup sugar
1 tablespoon lard or shortening

BATTER (mix in a bowl until smooth)†

> *½ cup water chestnut powder, sifted*
> *1 ¼ cups cold water*

DIRECTIONS FOR COOKING

1. Grease an 8-inch baking pan with oil.
2. In a medium-sized pot, place minced water chestnuts, ½ cup water, and lard or shortening. Bring to a boil. Pour in about a third of the batter and stir constantly over low heat until it bubbles. Remove from heat. Wait for about 2 minutes, then stir in the remaining batter and mix well. Pour contents in the oiled pan.
3. Cover and steam for about 30 minutes (see steaming instructions, page 184). Cool at room temperature or in the refrigerator. Slice into diamond pieces. Serve at room temperature.

DEEP-FRIED CRISP BANANA ROLLS
MAI LEUNG

Makes 20

PREPARATION OF INGREDIENTS

SESAME-COCONUT-SUGAR POWDER

> ½ cup sesame seeds
> 1 cup powdered sugar
> ½ cup sweetened flaked coconut

10 ripe bananas: peel, and slice into thin rounds
20 spring roll skins
2 egg yolks
oil for deep-frying

DIRECTIONS FOR COOKING

1. Heat sesame seeds in a small ungreased pot over low heat, stirring constantly, until they turn golden. Remove from heat and cool at room temperature. Crush sesame seeds coarsely with a rolling pin or grind them slightly in a spice or nut grinder. (The food processor cannot do this job.) Combine crushed sesame seeds, powdered sugar, and coconut flakes in a serving bowl. (This may be prepared days in advance and refrigerated in a covered jar. Bring it back to room temperature before use.)

2. Put banana slices (about half a banana for each roll) on a spring roll skin. Wrap as illustrated (opposite page), and seal with egg yolks. Prepare the others in the same manner. They can be prepared hours or a day in advance prior to this step. Put in plastic bag and refrigerate them until use.

3. Heat oil to deep-fry temperature (375 degrees). Deep-fry stuffed rolls until golden brown, then roll them on paper towels to drain off oil. Sprinkle each roll with sesame-coconut-sugar powder. Serve hot.

NOODLE DISHES

(For Lunch, Snack, or Evening Meal)

CHINESE NOODLES

The Chinese are certain that Marco Polo brought noodles from China and introduced them as spaghetti to the West. The Italians, of course, declare that they already had spaghetti long before Marco Polo's time. As a Chinese, I like to think we invented everything, including ravioli, which we call wonton. In the course of reading through three volumes of *The Travels of Marco Polo, the Venetian* (translated and edited by William Marsden, 1948), I did not find a single word about noodles, spaghetti, pasta, or anything remotely similar. I do not wish to join in this quarrel, choosing instead a seat on a fence post to watch the outcome.

I do hope that the quarrel will make one thing clear: the Chinese eat not only rice but also noodles, with as much passion as the Italians have for their pasta. Rice is not the national staple of all of China but only the South, the primary staple in the North being noodles. In the North, rice is served only on occasion. Noodles of great variety cooked in numberless ways, along with bread, compose most of the daily meals. Often breakfast is a bowl of piping hot noodles, a virtual necessity for warmth, since Chinese houses are not equipped with central heat. In the South, noodles are the secondary staple, commonly favored as lunch, afternoon or late evening snacks. And throughout China, great long noodles are eaten at the end of a birthday dinner to symbolize longevity.

Noodles are especially popular in China because they make a good one-dish meal. A housewife can save time preparing a large noodle dish, combining vegetables with meat or seafood to feed her entire family without cooking a few dishes plus rice. Also, noodle dishes use less meat and are therefore less expensive. By adding more noodles, vegetables, and sauce, you can stretch a meal to feed as many as you wish.

There are many small noodle restaurants in China as well as in Chinatowns in this country. The menus consist mainly of dozens of noodle dishes, prepared in countless ways with various kinds of noodles and ingredients. Some of them draw crowds to their doors, because the Chinese are discriminating noodle eaters. Our teeth are as sensitive as the ears of a devoted music lover, following wherever good noodles go. In Kowloon, Hong Kong, a small grubby place named Mark Chun Kee has been famous for its noodles for generations. There you can see chefs in undershirts cooking in full view of the customers, waiters yelling out orders across the floor, while housewives, coolies, students, and movie stars with dark glasses jam together hovering over dishes of noodles, oblivious of the hungry crowd watching and waiting over their shoulders. And there I also stood patiently in line, on my first day returning to Hong Kong last summer, for my bowl of those delicious noodles.

Homemade Noodles

Homemade noodles are delicious and not difficult to make, whether they are made by hand or by noodle machine. All it requires is a little of your time and hands that like to feel and touch. If you are among those who are convinced that anything dealing with dough will turn out disastrously for you, I still do not give up on you. Because each recipe makes a moderate amount of noodles, but enough for a dish that serves four as a meal, it is not something that will take hours, mess up the entire kitchen, or utterly exhaust you at the end. The whole process from beginning to cooking the noodles takes about 45 minutes altogether. If you have a noodle machine, it is even easier. Besides, noodles can be made and steamed a day or two in advance.

The Chinese noodlemaking process is similar to and yet quite different from that of other countries. Flour and eggs or flour and water are the basic ingredients. Sometimes chicken broth and shrimp roe are added to enhance flavor.

For noodles made by hand, the main tools are a rolling pin and a smooth sturdy work surface—wood is the best.

The Chinese rolling pin looks much like a French one, but shorter. A smooth wooden stick, it is 1½ inches in diameter and from 12 to 16 inches long.

Do not believe that a rolling pin has to be long and heavy. Because people differ so much in size, height and weight, pick one that suits you most comfortably. If it is awkwardly long, or clumsily wide, ask a carpenter to shorten it or shave it.

A new one should be rubbed with vegetable oil before use: wet your hands with a small amount of oil, and rub it several times periodically until the wood loses its rawness. To clean your rolling pin, do not immerse it in water, but wipe it with a damp sponge.

If you rub the dough as directed in the recipes, machine-made noodles are as good as hand-made ones. For making noodles by machine, I suggest the portable machines available in this country. Chinese noodle machines are too large for family use. They are usually owned by restaurants or noodle shops.

FRESH EGG NOODLES (MADE BY HAND)

Makes 10 ounces

Noodles made with flour and eggs alone are considered superior to those moistened with water in addition to the eggs. However, if you do not wish to make your own, they can be obtained in Chinese grocery stores and some of your local supermarkets. They are freshly made daily in Chinatowns.

PREPARATION OF INGREDIENTS

1 ¼ cups all-purpose flour: sift
2 medium-sized eggs: beat to mix yolks and whites thoroughly
cornstarch for dusting

DIRECTIONS FOR COOKING

1. In a mixing bowl, combine flour and beaten eggs. Use your hands to form a loose dough. Pick up a lump of dough and rub it vigorously between your hands. This will release the gluten from the flour, which will give the noodles some springiness when you bite into them. This quality is very important in Chinese cooking. It is what the Chinese call *sonng* (爽), a word for which there is no precise English equivalent. The opposite of *sonng* would be mushy, or inappropriately soft. *Sonng* is a combination of springiness, crunchiness, and a little resilience felt between one's teeth as one bites into well-prepared noodles or shrimp. Repeat until the remaining dough has been rubbed in the same manner.

2. Wash and dry hands, then turn dough on a floured working surface. Knead dough with the base of your hand until it is smooth and elastic. If the dough is too stiff, wet your hands with water and knead the dough to soften it.

3. Put dough in a lightly floured plastic bag and let it rest at room temperature for about 15 minutes.

4. Dust work surface with flour. Roll dough into a sausage and

divide it into four equal sections. Take up one section, covering the other three. Roll dough in your palms to form a round ball, then flatten it with one hand. With a rolling pin, roll dough from its center—away from you, then toward you—in a sweeping motion, using the strength of your arms, not the weight of your body. Roll dough until it becomes a paper-thin oval sheet.

5. Put a dry linen or terrycloth towel along the edge of a table. Dust noodle sheet lightly with cornstarch. Hang sheet by putting one-third of its length on the towel, and let the other two-thirds hang down. Stretch noodle sheet by pressing the end that is on the towel with one hand, and pull the other end downward with the other hand to the thinness you desire. Repeat with the other sheets in the same manner. Allow them to dry for about 15 minutes before cutting. (Do not overdry them. The right time to cut a noodle sheet is immediately after all four sheets are rolled, without intermission.)

6. Take the sheet that was rolled first and dust it with cornstarch. Fold sheet loosely from the narrow end until it is about 3 inches wide. With a Chinese cleaver press evenly and firmly on folded noodle sheet and cut it as thin as possible. Loosen noodles by holding one end up and letting it uncoil to drop gently on a surface dusted with cornstarch. Spread noodles loosely on a large tray.

7. For noodles in soup, do not leave the noodles in one batch. Rather, divide them into six portions, picking up each portion between the ends of your fingers and winding it into a small mound. Cover. The noodles are ready to be used in required recipe(s).

For fried noodles, it is not necessary to separate them into mounds. Just collect them gently into a loose batch.

FRESH EGG NOODLES
(MADE BY NOODLE MACHINE)

Makes 10 ounces

PREPARATION OF INGREDIENTS

1 ¼ cups all-purpose flour: sift
2 medium-sized eggs: beat to mix yolks and whites thoroughly
cornstarch for dusting

DIRECTIONS FOR COOKING

1. Prepare dough as in previous recipe from steps 1 through 3.

2. Dust work surface with flour. Roll dough into a sausage. Divide dough into four equal sections. Take up one section, covering the other three. Roll dough in your palms to form a round ball, then press to flatten it.

3. Feed flattened dough through the rollers to thin out dough, from the widest setting to the thinnest setting. Fold dough in half after going through each setting, except the thinnest setting.

4. When dough is fed through the thinnest setting, a very thin noodle sheet will come out. Lay noodle sheet flat between linen towels. Prepare the other three noodle sheets in the same manner.

5. Dust a noodle sheet with cornstarch and feed it through the finest cutting blade for thinnest noodles. Collect noodles gently and spread loosely on a tray that is dusted with cornstarch. Repeat dusting and cutting the other sheets in the same manner.

6. For noodles in soup, do not leave noodles in one batch; rather, divide them into six portions, picking up each portion between the ends of your fingers and winding it into a small mound. Cover. The noodles are ready to be used in required recipe(s).

For fried noodles, it is not necessary to separate them into mounds. Just collect them gently into a loose batch.

How to Keep Noodles Fresh, the Chinese Way
(Steamed Homemade Noodles)

If you want to make noodles in advance and keep them fresh, the best way is to steam them either by the batch or in mounds. Put the batch or mounds in an oiled steamer and steam for 10 minutes. The mounds should be separated from each other.

It is important that noodles and the water be a few inches away from each other, so that the noodles will not be dampened by the water.

Allow noodles to cool, then put in a 150-degree oven for about 20 minutes to dry thoroughly; cool before putting in a plastic bag. They keep well in the refrigerator for weeks.

How to Cook Noodles

There are three things many people overcook in this country: shrimp, vegetables, and noodles. I have already given detailed instructions on these in *The Classic Chinese Cookbook*. Since "good words never hurt to hear twice," I do not hesitate to repeat them again.

Fresh thin noodles are cooked in seconds. Please believe it. Noodles' sizes and kinds vary, and no teacher can tell you exactly how many seconds of cooking they need to be perfectly done. So the word "about" is going to be used frequently. But in general, it is preferable to undercook them rather than overcook them— most of them have to be recooked with meat and other ingredients.

The noodles in these recipes are based on the homemade Fresh Egg Noodles (pages 139 and 141) or fresh egg noodles bought in Chinatown. And please do not substitute domestic dried noodles or spaghetti or the dish will lose its authenticity.

Before cooking noodles, be sure you have a large colander or a large Chinese drainer. If not, you surely need one.

PLAIN NOODLES (COLD OR HOT)

Only 8 to 10 ounces of noodles are used here. If you need to double the noodles, be sure to double the water, salt, and oil too.

2 teaspoons salt
4 quarts water, in a large pot
8 to 10 ounces fresh egg noodles
½ cup cold water
2 tablespoons oil

DIRECTIONS FOR COOKING

1. Place colander in sink under faucet.

2. Add salt to 4 quarts of water and bring to a rapid boil over medium heat. Add noodles. Stir to separate immediately. Allow noodles to stay in water for about 15 seconds. Pour in ½ cup cold water.

3. For cold noodles: Quickly pour noodles into colander and immediately run cold tap water over them thoroughly, tossing them with chopsticks or a fork to prevent further cooking. When noodles are no longer warm to touch, shake them in the colander for several seconds. Add oil. Toss to coat them evenly. The oil is to keep them from sticking to each other. Spread on a plate. These cold noodles are ready to be used in the required recipes.

4. For hot noodles: Quickly pour noodles into colander. Shake to drain off water. Add oil, tossing to coat noodles evenly. Since the noodles are still cooking by their own heat, it is better to use them as soon as possible or cook them just before you need them.

NOODLE NESTS FLAVORED WITH SHRIMP
ROE OR CHICKEN

Makes 10 noodle nests (1 pound noodles)

Shrimp roe are the Chinese gourmet's delight. They might not excite your palate (just as many Chinese feel lukewarm about caviar), but they add a delicate shrimp flavor to these noodles, and we love their exquisite taste. Shrimp roe are available in Chinese supermarkets for about five dollars an ounce. They are dark rust in color and tiny like fine sand. If you have not developed a love for them, you may omit them and make these noodles with only chicken flavor.

In China, noodles flavored with shrimp roe or chicken are always made into dried noodle nests for later use as quick meals. When we are hungry but short of time, we simply put a couple of these noodle nests into boiling good broth for about a minute, add whatever green vegetable or leftover meat we have, and we have a delicious wholesome hot lunch or snack. Or, we toss the boiled noodles with scallions, ginger, a little oil, and oyster sauce, and this is delicious too. The cooking is so simple and fast that even children can do it.

Now, various kinds of instant noodles made in the Orient are available in American supermarkets. With preservatives added and powdered stock included in each package, they are a sort of Oriental junk food. I hoped I would never see the Chinese eat their meals out of paper boxes. My heart and spirit were low and dark as the Ninth Hell when I recently saw that Hong Kong was full of McDonald's hamburgers. And people ate standing, right out of paper cartons, in hundreds of fast-food stores. Where are we hurrying to?

PREPARATION OF INGREDIENTS

1 tablespoon dried shrimp roe
⅓ cup condensed chicken broth
2 chicken bouillon cubes
1 egg
4 teaspoons salt
4 teaspoons sugar
2 cups all-purpose flour
cornstarch for dusting

DIRECTIONS FOR COOKING

1. Heat shrimp roe in a small pot over low heat, stirring constantly for about a minute or until they are slightly roasted. Cool at room temperature.

2. Pour chicken broth in a small pot; cover and heat over low heat. When it begins to boil, turn off heat and add bouillon cubes. Stir to dissolve. Cool.

3. In a large mixing bowl, beat egg, salt, sugar, and cooled broth thoroughly; add roasted shrimp roe and mix well.

4. Sift flour into liquid mixture and mix with hand to form a rough dough. Prepare and make noodles as in the recipes for Fresh Egg Noodles, either by hand or with a portable noodle machine, following steps 2 to 6 inclusive if made by hand; 2 to 5 if made by machine.

5. Divide noodles into ten equal mounds. Fold and tuck each mound into a small nest.

6. Put noodle nests (separated from each other) on an oiled steamer basket or perforated tray. Cover and steam over high heat for 10 minutes. Transfer noodle nests to a rack, and put in a low oven (150 to 175 degrees) to dry thoroughly. It will take about 20 minutes.

7. Cool dried noodle nests before putting in plastic bags or covered jars. They will keep well for months in the refrigerator.

SUMMER COLD SPICED NOODLES, SZECHWAN STYLE

Serves 12 to 15 as an appetizer, 6 as a meal

This large platter of spicy noodles topped with succulent shrimp, lean pork strips, crispy celery, scallions, and other ingredients is an excellent summer dish or peppy appetizer for all seasons. Also, it can be prepared hours in advance.

PREPARATION OF INGREDIENTS

1 pound fresh egg noodles: cook as in Plain Noodles (Cold) (see page 143)
2 slices fresh ginger root, the size of a quarter
4 cups water
2 tablespoons pale dry sherry or white wine
1 pound medium-sized shrimp in shells
12 ounces lean pork or boned, skinned chicken breasts: steam for 15 minutes, cool, cut into thin strips
1½ cups celery in thin strips 1½ inches long
½ cup red bell pepper in thin strips (discard seeds and ribs)
1 cup shredded scallions in 1½-inch length, including some green
¼ pound jellyfish skin (optional): rinse off salt, soak in plenty of cold water for at least 4 hours, immerse in a pot of boiling water, and rinse in cold water at once; cut into thin strips (can be kept in refrigerator a day or more)
2 ounces Szechwan mustard pickles (optional): rinse, mince, soak in a large bowl of cold water for about 15 minutes, squeeze off water

SAUCE MIXTURE (mix in a bowl)

1 tablespoon minced fresh ginger root
1 tablespoon minced garlic
4 teaspoons sugar
½ teaspoon flower peppercorn powder
6 tablespoons black soy sauce

3 tablespoons Chenkong vinegar or red rice vinegar
3 tablespoons sesame oil
1 teaspoon chili oil

DIRECTIONS FOR COOKING

1. Spread cooked cold noodles on a large platter. Cover and put aside.

2. Add ginger to 4 cups water and bring to a rapid boil. Add wine, immediately drop in the shrimp, and count 35 seconds. Turn off heat. Quickly remove shrimp with a drainer and cool in refrigerator. Peel off shells and devein. Cover and refrigerate shrimp.

3. Arrange shrimp, shredded cooked pork or chicken, celery, pepper, scallions, and jellyfish skin shreds (they may be grouped or mixed together) on noodles; sprinkle Szechwan mustard pickles on top.

4. Just before serving, stir and mix sauce mixture well. Pour sauce evenly over above ingredients on platter. Serve cold or at room temperature.

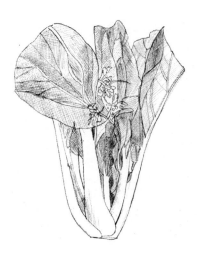

SESAME CHICKEN SHRED NOODLES, PEKING FLAVOR

Serves 6 as a meal

This colorful dish can be doubled or tripled and prepared in advance. It delights the palate and pleases the eyes. It makes an elegant meal for large gatherings, even more so if it is accompanied by the hot crescents or turnovers in this book.

PREPARATION OF INGREDIENTS

8 to 10 ounces fresh egg noodles: cook as in Plain Noodles (Cold), page 143
1 cup Chinese celery cabbage, cut crosswise in thin strips
6 bay leaves
4 quarts water
3 chicken breasts (about 3 pounds): cut each in half
¼ cup red bell pepper in pea-sized pieces
¼ cup snipped parsley
¼ cup sesame seeds: stir and roast in an ungreased small pot over low heat until golden brown, cool before use
1 tablespoon sesame oil
3 tablespoons peanut or vegetable oil

SEASONINGS (put in a bowl)†

¼ teaspoon flower peppercorn powder
¼ teaspoon cayenne pepper
2 dried chili peppers: tear into small pieces (use seeds also)
2 teaspoons minced garlic
1 tablespoon minced fresh ginger root
¼ cup scallions in pea-sized pieces, including some green

SAUCE MIXTURE (mix in a blender or food processor or by hand)†

2 tablespoons sugar
6 tablespoons black soy sauce
4 teaspoons Chinese red vinegar
2 teaspoons sesame paste or peanut butter

DIRECTIONS FOR COOKING

1. Spread cooked cold noodles on a large serving platter and sprinkle them with the celery cabbage. Cover with plastic wrap and set aside.

2. Put bay leaves and water in a large pot and bring to a rapid boil. Add chicken breasts. When water returns to a boil again, put lid on. Turn off heat; allow chicken breasts to poach in water for 20 minutes. Remove chicken breasts, drain, and cool in refrigerator.

3. Bone chicken breasts, and trim off excess skin (the Chinese love chicken skin, but if you dislike it, discard it). Cut chicken breasts crosswise into ½-inch strips and arrange them neatly on the celery cabbage and the noodles, then sprinkle them evenly with red bell pepper, parsley, and roasted sesame seeds.

4. Heat sesame oil and peanut or vegetable oil in a small pot over medium heat. When oil is hot, drop in the seasonings and brown them slightly. Stir in sauce mixture, and cook, stirring, until it begins to foam. Remove from heat. Pour sauce over chicken evenly just before serving. (You may cook the seasoned sauce in advance and keep in a covered jar until use.) Serve at room temperature.

TWO FACES YELLOW NOODLES, SHANGHAI STYLE

Serves 4 as a meal

Besides serving noodles soft or in soup, the Shanghainese pan-fry noodles the same way the Cantonese do: until the noodles are crisp outside but still soft inside. The Shanghainese call these noodles "Two Faces Yellow" because of their golden color on both sides. Like all noodle dishes, this one is good for a snack or lunch, and also wonderful to serve as dinner.

PREPARATION OF INGREDIENTS

1 cup oil
½ pound fresh egg noodles: cook as in Plain Noodles (Cold), page 143
2 teaspoons minced fresh ginger root
2 teaspoons minced garlic
½ cup scallions shredded in 1½-inch length, including some green
⅓ cup Chinese dried mushrooms: soak in hot water until spongy, discard stems, shred caps
2 cups shredded Chinese celery cabbage

SAUCE MIXTURE (mix in a bowl)†

    ¼ teaspoon salt
    ¼ teaspoon sugar
    ⅛ teaspoon ground white pepper
    2 tablespoons black soy sauce
    2 tablespoons pale dry sherry
    2 teaspoons sesame oil

1 cup chicken broth (not condensed) mixed with 4 teaspoons cornstarch

CHICKEN MIXTURE (put ingredients directly on chicken, mix, blanch chicken mixture in water: see page 192)

> *1½ boned skinned chicken breasts: cut into matchstick strips (to make 1 cup)*
> *⅛ teaspoon salt*
> *2 teaspoons cornstarch*
> *½ teaspoon soy sauce*
> *about ½ egg white*

Soy-Oil Dip (page 174) and a small dish of Chinese chili sauce or Tabasco sauce

DIRECTIONS FOR COOKING

1. Heat wok over high heat. Swirl in 1 cup oil. When oil is hot but not smoking, spread noodles evenly on bottom of wok. Pan-fry noodles over medium heat until golden brown on bottom. Turn noodles, and pan-fry until the other side is also golden brown. Remove from wok to an ovenproof plate or tray. Place in a 300-degree oven to keep them hot and crisp.

2. Remove all but 3 tablespoons oil from wok. Heat oil over high heat, and add ginger, garlic, scallions, and mushrooms. Stir-fry until garlic turns golden. Add celery cabbage. Stir-fry for about 15 seconds. Stir and swirl in sauce mixture. When sauce begins to bubble gently, stir in the broth with cornstarch. Stir and cook constantly until sauce is slightly thickened. Add chicken mixture and cook briskly to reheat.

3. Put noodles on a large serving platter and top with the chicken and cabbage mixture. Serve hot with dip and sauce.

BEEF WITH BLACK BEAN SAUCE
ON GOLDEN BROWN NOODLES

Serves 4 as a meal

PREPARATION OF INGREDIENTS

1 cup oil
10 ounces fresh egg noodles: cook as in Plain Noodles (Cold), page 143

BEEF MIXTURE (put ingredients directly on beef, mix, refrigerate until use)†

> *10 ounces flank steak: cut against grain into pieces ⅛ inch thick and 2 inches long*
> *1 teaspoon brown sugar*
> *2 tablespoons cornstarch*
> *1 tablespoon black soy sauce*
> *1 tablespoon sesame oil*

SEASONINGS (put on a plate)†

> *2 fresh or dried chili peppers: cut into small rings; if dried ones are used, tear them in small pieces by hand (use seeds if you prefer a hotter dish)*
> *1 tablespoon minced fresh ginger root*
> *1 tablespoon minced garlic*
> *3 tablespoons salted black beans: put in a tea drainer, run hot tap water on them for several seconds, mash into paste*

¼ pound fresh snow peas: snap off ends and any strings
1 bell pepper (preferably red): discard ribs and seeds, cut into ¼-inch strips
1 onion: peel and cut into thin strips

SAUCE MIXTURE (mix in a bowl)†

1 ½ cups clear chicken broth (not condensed)
1 teaspoon sugar
2 ½ tablespoons thin soy sauce
2 tablespoons cornstarch

DIRECTIONS FOR COOKING

1. Heat wok over high heat. Swirl in oil. When oil is hot, spread noodles evenly on bottom of wok. Pan-fry noodles over medium heat until golden brown on bottom. Turn noodles, and pan-fry until other side is also golden brown (but noodles are still soft inside). Remove from wok to an ovenproof plate or tray. Place in a 300-degree oven to keep hot and crisp.

2. Heat the oil remaining in wok to deep-fry temperature over medium heat. Add beef mixture; stir quickly to separate pieces. Blanch briskly until meat just loses its redness. Remove with a Chinese drainer or a large slotted spoon to a bowl.

3. Remove all but 2 tablespoons oil from wok. Heat oil over high heat, add seasonings, and stir to cook until garlic turns golden. Add snow peas, pepper, and onion, and stir-fry for about 10 seconds. Swirl in sauce mixture (stir well before adding). Stir and cook until sauce bubbles gently. Return beef (with juice) to wok. Mix well. Turn off heat.

4. Put fried noodles on a big serving platter and place the whole contents from wok on top. Serve hot at once.

Note: If a peppery dish is not desired, just omit the chili peppers. It is still delicious.

STIR-FRIED RICE NOODLES, SING CHOU STYLE

Serves 4 as a meal

Sing Chou is the Chinese name for Singapore, where many of our kin emigrated for centuries. For generations, this has been one of the favorite noodle dishes among many Chinese. We love the flavor of the curry paste that spices and jazzes up the noodles, and its aroma delights us with a whiff of the tropical.

You can find this dish easily in teahouses in this country as well as in the Orient.

PREPARATION OF INGREDIENTS

6 tablespoons oil
2 eggs: beat to combine yolks and whites well
1 teaspoon minced garlic
6 scallions: cut into 1½-inch lengths, shred, including some green
½ pound Chinese Barbecued Pork (page 118): cut into matchstick strips
8 Chinese dried mushrooms: soak in hot water until spongy, discard stems, shred caps

SHRIMP MIXTURE (mix in a bowl, refrigerate before use)†

   ½ pound fresh shrimp: shell, devein, rinse in cold water, pat dry, cut each into 4 thin strips
   ¼ teaspoon baking soda
   ⅓ egg white
   1 teaspoon sherry

⅓ cup bell pepper (preferably red) in long thin strips

SAUCE MIXTURE (mix in a bowl)†

1 tablespoon curry paste
1 teaspoon curry powder
¼ teaspoon cayenne pepper
½ teaspoon sugar
1 tablespoon black soy sauce
1 tablespoon thin soy sauce
1 tablespoon sherry

½ pound dried rice sticks; soak in very warm but not burning hot tap water for 15 minutes, or until they just soften but are still resistant (do not oversoak them); drain in colander; put in plastic bag to keep from drying
2 cups fresh bean sprouts: clean in cold water, drain
2 teaspoons sesame oil

DIRECTIONS FOR COOKING

1. Heat wok hot over medium heat. Swirl in 2 tablespoons oil. When oil is hot, swirl in eggs and spread into a large pancake. Turn pancake when it is set. Remove from wok when it is no longer running. Cut pancake into thin strips. Set aside.

2. Heat wok over high heat. Swirl in 4 tablespoons oil. When oil is hot, drop in the garlic. When it turns golden, add half the scallions and stir-fry for a few seconds. Add barbecued pork, then mushrooms, and stir-fry for about 20 seconds. Put in shrimp mixture, stir, and cook until shrimp just turns whitish. Add bell pepper. Immediately swirl in sauce mixture, mixing well. Turn heat to medium. Add rice sticks, toss, mix, and cook until they are evenly coated with sauce. Drop in bean sprouts. Toss and stir until rice sticks are thoroughly heated. Swirl in sesame oil. Add remaining scallions; mix well. Transfer to a large serving platter. Serve hot.

STIR-FRIED RICE NOODLES WITH BEEF, SATÉ FLAVOR

Serves 4 as a meal

Saté sauce is a Malayan-style sauce. It is hot and spicy, made with soy sauce, shrimp, chili, sugar, garlic, oil, and other spices. Some comes from Hong Kong (bottled by Amoy Canning Company) and some from Malaysia. It is available in Chinese grocery stores. It will keep for weeks in the refrigerator.

PREPARATION OF INGREDIENTS

⅓ cup oil

BEEF MIXTURE (put ingredients directly on beef; mix in a bowl)†

> *1 pound flank steak: cut against grain into thin strips 1 ½ inches long*
> *½ teaspoon sugar*
> *1 tablespoon cornstarch*
> *1 tablespoon mushroom soy or black soy sauce*
> *2 teaspoons sesame oil*

SAUCE MIXTURE (mix in a bowl)†

> *½ teaspoon sugar*
> *2 tablespoons Saté sauce*
> *5 teaspoons curry paste*
> *1 tablespoon thin soy sauce*
> *1 tablespoon sherry*

1 cup leeks or scallions in thin strips 1 ½ inches long
1 large red bell pepper: discard seeds and ribs, cut into thin long strips
½ pound dried rice sticks: soak in very warm (not burning hot) tap water for 15 minutes, or until they just soften (do not oversoak them), drain in colander, put in plastic bag to keep from drying
½ pound fresh bean sprouts: clean in cold water, drain

DIRECTIONS FOR COOKING

Heat wok hot over high heat and add oil. When oil is hot, add beef mixture, and stir quickly to separate pieces. When beef is still a little red, push it to one side of the wok and add the sauce mixture to the other side. Stir and cook until sauce begins to bubble; drop in leeks or scallions and red pepper. Combine all the ingredients in the wok. Add soaked rice sticks, stirring constantly until they are hot and evenly coated with sauce. Drop in the bean sprouts and stir continually for about a minute. Transfer to a serving platter. Serve hot.

SZECHWAN SPICED BEEF WITH
VEGETABLE ON NOODLES

Serves 6 as a meal

PREPARATION OF INGREDIENTS

6 tablespoons oil
1 tablespoon fresh ginger root
1 tablespoon minced garlic
½ cup chopped scallions, including some green

BEEF MIXTURE (mix in a bowl)†

   2 pounds stew beef chunks (use beef with a little fat): cut chunks into
      ¼-inch-thick pieces
   5 teaspoons Szechwan chili bean sauce
   2 ½ tablespoons Szechwan sweet bean sauce or ground bean sauce

SAUCE MIXTURE (mix in a bowl)†

   2 teaspoons sugar
   4 whole star anise
   4 tablespoons black soy sauce
   ½ teaspoon flower peppercorn powder (see page 171)

3 cups water
8 to 10 ounces fresh egg noodles: cook as Plain Noodles (Hot), page 143
½ pound fresh broccoli or yu choy: cut into finger-sized pieces, blanch in
   boiling water, drain

DIRECTIONS FOR COOKING

   1. Heat oil in a 4- to 6-quart pot. Add ginger, garlic, and half the scallions, and cook for a few seconds. Add beef mixture, and cook until beef loses its redness. Stir in sauce mixture and mix well. Add 2 cups water; cover and simmer for 1 hour. Add the remaining water and cook over low heat until beef is tender— about another hour. There should be 1½ cups sauce left in the pot when beef is done. Beef can be cooked a day or two in advance; reheat on stove over low heat.

2. Put hot noodles and blanched vegetable on a large platter and top with beef mixture and the remaining scallions. Serve hot.

SZECHWAN SPICY BEAN THREAD NOODLES IN SOUP

Serves 4 as a meal

PREPARATION OF INGREDIENTS

5 cups chicken or beef broth (homemade or canned, but not condensed)
2 to 3 ounces Szechwan mustard pickle (also called jah choy or preserved mustard): rinse off surface spice, mince coarsely (to make ½ cup)
½ cup golden mushrooms: rinse in cold water, drain
4 Chinese dried mushrooms: soak in hot water until spongy, discard stems, shred caps

BEEF MIXTURE (mix in a bowl)†

12 ounces lean beef: mince by hand or coarsely grind in food processor
¼ teaspoon ground pepper
½ teaspoon sugar
1 tablespoon Szechwan chili bean paste
1 tablespoon mushroom soy or black soy sauce
2 teaspoons sesame oil

4 ounces bean thread noodles: soak in a large bowl of warm water for 3 minutes, drain in a colander
a handful of fresh snow peas (pinch off ends) or fresh peas from pods
¼ cup chopped scallions, including some green

DIRECTIONS FOR COOKING

In a 3-quart pot or Chinese clay pot, bring broth to a rapid boil; add mustard pickle, golden mushrooms, and soaked dried mushrooms. Cover and simmer for about 3 minutes. Stir in beef mixture and cook until it loses its redness. Add noodles and bring to a boil. (Do not overcook noodles—they become mushy easily.) Immerse peas in broth and cook for about 1 minute. Turn off heat; add scallions. Serve hot.

SILK THREADS FROM HEAVEN

(STIR-FRIED SHREDDED PORK WITH VEGETABLES ON BEAN THREAD NOODLES)

Serves 4 to 5 as a meal

PREPARATION OF INGREDIENTS

4 cups oil
2 ounces bean thread noodles
2 eggs with ⅛ teaspoon salt: beat well to mix yolk and white
1 teaspoon minced garlic
½ cup shredded scallions, including some green

PORK MIXTURE (put ingredients directly on pork and mix in a bowl)†

> *1 pound lean pork: cut into matchstick strips (to make 2 cups)*
> *⅛ teaspoon salt*
> *½ teaspoon sugar*
> *¼ teaspoon white pepper*
> *2 teaspoons cornstarch*
> *1 teaspoon sesame oil*
> *2 teaspoons thin soy sauce*

VEGETABLES (put on a plate)†

> *½ cup Chinese dried mushrooms: soak in hot water until spongy, discard stems, shred caps*
> *½ cup shredded salted mustard greens: soak in 2 cups cold water for 10 minutes, squeeze off water*
> *2 cups shredded celery, in 1½-inch matchstick strips*
> *1 cup shredded bamboo shoots, in 1½-inch matchstick strips*
> *¼ cup shredded red bell pepper, in matchstick strips*

SAUCE MIXTURE (mix in a bowl)†

> *2 tablespoons black soy sauce*
> *1 tablespoon sherry*
> *½ teaspoon sugar*
> *1 tablespoon sesame oil*
> *¼ teaspoon salt*
> *2 teaspoons cornstarch*
> *¼ cup chicken broth*

DIRECTIONS FOR COOKING

1. Heat oil in wok to deep-fry temperature (375 degrees). Pull and separate noodles into two portions. Then again pull to loosen each portion. Test oil by dropping in a piece of noodle; if it pops up instantly, the oil is right. Immerse noodles into oil; the noodles immediately turn into a white nest. Turn nest over and fry the other side. (This procedure takes only a few seconds.) Drain on paper towels. The noodles can be fried hours in advance; cool and put in a plastic bag.

2. Remove oil from wok except about 2 tablespoons. Turn heat to medium. When oil is hot, pour in the eggs. Slowly swirl the eggs by turning the wok clockwise to form a large pancake. Turn pancake over when it is no longer runny. When it is set, transfer to a cutting board. Cut pancake into thin strips. Put aside.

3. Heat wok over high heat. Swirl in 4 tablespoons oil. When oil is hot, drop in garlic and half the scallions. As soon as garlic turns light gold, add pork mixture. Stir-fry until pork loses its pink. Add mushrooms, stir, and cook for about 15 seconds; put in the vegetables; mix and stir well. As soon as the celery begins to soften, swirl in sauce mixture. Stir constantly until sauce thickens. Turn off heat.

4. Put fried noodles on a large platter, and transfer contents of the wok onto noodles. Top it with egg shreds and the remaining scallions. Serve hot.

SNOW CABBAGE, PORK SHREDS, AND BEAN THREAD NOODLES IN SOUP

Serves 3 as a meal

PREPARATION OF INGREDIENTS

3 tablespoons oil
4 scallions: cut into pea-sized pieces, including some green

PORK MIXTURE (mix in a bowl)†

  about 8 ounces lean pork: cut into matchstick strips (to make 1 cup)
  1 teaspoon black soy sauce
  1 tablespoon cornstarch

1 cup bamboo shoots in matchstick strips
½ cup canned snow cabbage (loosely packed): drain off juice

SAUCE MIXTURE (mix in a bowl)†

  ⅛ teaspoon ground white pepper
  ½ teaspoon sugar
  1 tablespoon thin soy sauce
  1 teaspoon sherry

BROTH (mix in a pot)†

  4 cups clear chicken broth (not condensed)
  ½ teaspoon salt

4 ounces bean thread noodles: soak in hot water for 15 minutes, drain in
  colander, cut noodles short with scissors
2 teaspoons sesame oil

DIRECTIONS FOR COOKING

1. Heat wok over high heat until it is hot. Swirl in 3 tablespoons oil. When oil is hot, drop in half the scallions and add pork mixture. Stir-fry until pork loses its pink color. Add bamboo shoots and snow cabbage. Stir-fry for about 30 seconds. Stir in

sauce mixture. Stir and cook for 30 seconds. Turn off heat. Cover to keep hot.

2. Bring broth to a rapid boil. Add bean thread noodles. When broth comes to a boil again, turn off heat.

3. Put noodles in individual serving bowls. Top noodles with pork mixture. Garnish each bowl with sesame oil and remaining scallions. Pour broth into each bowl. Serve hot.

NOODLES IN MEAT SAUCE, PEKING STYLE

Serves 4 as a meal

PREPARATION OF INGREDIENTS

3 tablespoons oil
2 teaspoons minced garlic
½ cup chopped scallions, including some green
1 pound pork (with 10 to 15 percent fat): grind coarsely in a meat grinder
* or food processor*

SAUCE MIXTURE (mix in a bowl)†

* 4 tablespoons Szechwan sweet bean sauce or ground bean sauce*
* 1 teaspoon sugar*
* 2 tablespoons Chinese Shaohsing wine or sake or sherry*

½ cup clear chicken broth (not condensed)
1 tablespoon sesame oil
4 quarts water
2 teaspoons salt
10 to 12 ounces fresh egg noodles

DIRECTIONS FOR COOKING

1. Heat wok over high heat. Swirl in 2 tablespoons oil. When oil is hot, drop in garlic and half the scallions. When garlic turns golden, add ground pork. Stir-fry until pork loses its pink. Stir in sauce mixture; stir and cook for about 2 minutes. Add the broth.

Mix well. Simmer over low heat for about 7 minutes, stirring constantly. Add sesame oil and mix well. Cover to keep hot, or reheat just before serving.

2. Bring 4 quarts of water to rapid boil. Add the salt and then the noodles. Stir immediately: they are done in less than 30 seconds, before the water returns to a boil. It is better to undercook than overcook them.

3. Quickly pour noodles into a colander. Shake the colander to drain off water. Add 1 tablespoon oil to toss and coat noodles evenly. Put on a serving platter and top with the meat sauce and the remaining scallions. Serve hot at once.

BEEF WITH SAH HO RICE NOODLES

Serves 3 to 4 as a meal

Sah Ho is a small area in Kwangchow, China, where these noodles originated. These fresh soft, white, wide noodles are made with rice powder daily by noodle shops in marketplaces and in Chinatown. Few Chinese families make their own because of the equipment involved. They come in a large round sheet and are already thoroughly cooked. Each sheet weighs about a pound, and usually comes uncut and folded for easy handling. Cut it into ½-inch-wide strips before using it.

These noodles are very white, smooth, and flimsy; unusual by Western standards, but absolutely delicious.

PREPARATION OF INGREDIENTS

1 cup oil

BEEF MIXTURE (combine and refrigerate until use)†

> *12 ounces flank steak: cut against the grain into pieces ⅛ inch thick and 2 inches long*
> *1 teaspoon brown sugar*

1 tablespoon cornstarch
1 tablespoon black soy sauce
2 teaspoons sherry
2 teaspoons sesame oil

1 teaspoon minced fresh ginger root
1 teaspoon minced garlic
½ cup scallions in 1½-inch lengths, including some green
⅓ cup green or red bell pepper strips

SAUCE MIXTURE (mix in a bowl)†

¼ teaspoon salt
¼ teaspoon sugar
2 tablespoons black soy sauce

1 pound Sah Ho rice noodles, in ½-inch-wide strips
2 cups fresh bean sprouts
Soy-Oil Dip (page 174) and a small dish of Chinese chili sauce or Tabasco sauce

DIRECTIONS FOR COOKING

1. Heat wok over high heat. Swirl in oil. When oil is hot (but not smoking), add beef mixture. Stir quickly to separate pieces, and blanch briskly until meat just loses its redness. Remove beef from wok with a Chinese drainer or a large slotted spoon, and put in a bowl.

2. Remove all but 3 tablespoons oil from wok. Heat oil over medium heat, and add ginger, garlic, scallions, and pepper. Stir-fry for about 10 seconds. Swirl in sauce mixture and stir quickly for few seconds; return beef (with juice) to wok and mix briskly. Add rice noodles; stir and toss gently until noodles are evenly coated with sauce. Drop in the bean sprouts. Stir and toss constantly until noodles are hot. Put on a platter. Serve hot with dip and sauce.

SAH HO RICE NOODLES WITH
PORK SHREDS AND BEAN SPROUTS

Serves 3 as a meal

PREPARATION OF INGREDIENTS

5 tablespoons oil
6 scallions: cut into 1½-inch lengths, including some green
6 Chinese dried mushrooms: soak in hot water until spongy, discard stems, shred caps
12 ounces lean pork: cut into matchstick strips
½ pound fresh bean sprouts: wash and drain

SAUCE MIXTURE (mix in a bowl)†

> *¾ teaspoon salt*
> *¼ teaspoon sugar*
> *4 teaspoons black soy sauce*
> *1 teaspoon thin soy sauce*
> *2 teaspoons sherry*

1 pound Sah Ho rice noodles, in ½-inch-wide strips

DIRECTIONS FOR COOKING

Heat wok over high heat. Swirl in oil. When oil is hot, drop in half the scallions and add the mushrooms; stir-fry for about 30 seconds. Add pork strips and cook until they are no longer pink. Add bean sprouts, then stir in sauce mixture. Stir and cook for about 20 seconds. Add the rice noodles. Stir-fry gently over medium heat until the noodles are just heated through. Add the remaining scallions. Put on a serving platter. Serve hot.

SIMPLE PLEASURE NOODLES

Serves 2

PREPARATION OF INGREDIENTS

2 tablespoons lard or peanut oil
2 teaspoons minced fresh ginger root
¼ cup oyster sauce
1 teaspoon sesame oil (optional)
5 homemade Noodle Nests Flavored with Shrimp Roe or Chicken (page 144) or 4 ounces fresh egg noodles
¼ pound Chinese Barbecued Pork (page 118) or cooked ham (sandwich ham can be used): slice into bite-sized pieces
½ cup scallions in 1½-inch-long thin strips, including some green

DIRECTIONS FOR COOKING

1. Heat lard or oil in a small pot over medium heat. When it is hot, drop in ginger. When ginger turns golden, stir in oyster sauce; stir and cook over low heat until sauce begins to bubble. Turn off heat, add sesame oil, and cover to keep hot.

2. Bring 4 quarts of water to a rapid boil. Add noodle nests and loosen them with a pair of chopsticks or fork. As soon as the nests come loose and the water comes to a full boil, pour noodles in a colander and shake to drain off water. Put noodles on a serving plate, and top off with barbecued pork or ham and scallions. Toss with heated oyster sauce. Serve hot.

SAUCES AND DIPS

CHILI OIL

Makes about 1 ½ cups

Chili oil can be obtained in Chinese grocery stores, but very often it tastes like a chemical, and sometimes it's too mild. It is best to make it yourself. This chili oil is very hot, and should be used according to your taste.

PREPARATION OF INGREDIENTS

2 cups peanut or corn oil
1 ½ cups dried red chili peppers: tear or chop into small pieces, do not discard seeds
5 teaspoons cayenne pepper

DIRECTIONS FOR COOKING

1. Heat oil in a small pot over medium-low heat. The oil should be hot, but not yet to deep-fry temperature. (Test by dropping a pepper in the oil; if pepper sizzles gently, then the oil is right. If pepper turns black quickly, the oil is too hot; cool it down before adding the rest of the peppers.) Add peppers and their seeds. Cover and cook gently over low heat, stirring from time to time, until all the peppers turn black. Turn off heat and let oil cool a little, about 15 minutes, before adding cayenne. (If oil is too hot, it will burn the cayenne.)
2. Add cayenne, stir, and mix well. Cover and let chili oil stand at room temperature overnight.
3. Strain chili oil, which is orange-red in color, through cheesecloth into a jar. Cover and keep in refrigerator—it will last indefinitely. (Although chili oil becomes cloudy in the refrigerator, it will clear up quickly at room temperature.)

FIVE-FRAGRANCE SALT DIP

Makes about ⅓ cup

6 tablespoons salt
¼ teaspoon five-fragrance powder
½ teaspoon ground pepper

Heat a small pot over medium heat until it is hot. Add salt and stir constantly. When salt is very hot, add five-fragrance powder and pepper. Mix well and turn off heat. Cool; put the dip in a covered jar. It will keep for months. Use it sparingly. Put a small amount into small dishes and serve as a dip. It is also very good to use as a table salt.

FLOWER PEPPERCORN POWDER

Makes about ⅓ cup

6 tablespoons flower peppercorns, or more

Heat a small pot over medium heat until it is hot. Add flower peppercorns. Stir constantly until peppercorns turn deep brown and become aromatic. (They smoke slightly.) Remove from heat.
Grind roasted peppercorns to a powder in a pepper mill. Put the powder in a covered jar. It will keep for months.

FLOWER PEPPERCORN AND SALT DIP

Makes about ⅓ cup

2 teaspoons flower peppercorn powder (see preceding recipe)
4 tablespoons salt
1 teaspoon ground pepper

Mix all the ingredients. Store in a covered jar; it will keep for months. Use sparingly. Put a small amount into small dishes and serve as a dip.

FRESH CHILI PEPPER-SOY-VINEGAR DIP

Makes about ½ cup

⅓ cup red vinegar
¼ cup black soy sauce
1 fresh chili pepper: cut into small rounds; use the seeds if you prefer a
  hotter dip
1 tablespoon peanut or corn oil

Combine vinegar, soy sauce, and chili pepper (with or without seeds) in a serving bowl. Heat oil until it is hot and pour over mixture.

GINGER-SOY-VINEGAR DIP

Makes about ½ cup

¼ cup finely shredded fresh ginger root
¼ cup Chinese red vinegar
2 tablespoons black soy sauce

Mix in a serving bowl; cover and allow to stand at room temperature for at least 10 minutes before serving. It will keep for hours at room temperature.

MUSTARD-OIL DIP

Makes about 4 servings

Mustard will lose its flavor and strength if it is prepared too far in advance. It is best to make this dip within half an hour before serving.

2 tablespoons Colman's mustard powder
1 teaspoon sesame oil

Mix mustard with enough water to make a thin paste. Then put it in a serving bowl and top with sesame oil.

OYSTER-OIL DIP

Makes about ⅓ cup

2 tablespoons lard or oil
¼ cup oyster sauce

Heat lard or oil and oyster sauce in a small pot over low heat until it just begins to bubble. Put in a serving dish. Serve either hot or at room temperature.

PLUM SAUCE DIP

Makes about ⅔ cup

about 3 tablespoons water
½ cup canned plum sauce

Mix water with plum sauce until consistency is that of heavy syrup. Put in container and refrigerate. Serve at room temperature.

SESAME PASTE

Makes about ½ cup

½ cup sesame seeds
2 teaspoons sesame oil

Heat a small pot over medium heat until it is hot. Add sesame seeds, and stir constantly until sesame seeds turn golden. Remove from heat and cool to room temperature.

Put roasted sesame seeds and oil in a grinder and grind to a paste. Put in a covered jar.

SOY-OIL DIP

Makes about ¼ cup

4 tablespoons black soy sauce
1 tablespoon sesame oil or peanut oil

Put soy sauce in a serving bowl. Heat oil until it is hot and pour over soy sauce.

SOY-VINEGAR DIP

Makes about ⅓ cup

¼ cup Chinese red vinegar
2 tablespoons black soy sauce

Mix in a serving bowl and serve.

CHINESE TEA

ON DRINKING TEA

China introduced tea to the world. Tea cultivation is said to have been begun about four thousand years ago by Shen Nung (Divine Farmer), China's second mythical emperor. His mother conceived him by the spirit of a dragon. He was born with the head of a bull and the body of a man. He spoke in three days, walked in a week, and plowed the fields when he was three. His divine mission was to teach man to farm, to yoke the ox, to saddle the horse, to cultivate fine grains. Shen Nung was credited with tasting and categorizing 365 species of plants and herbs, and among them was tea. He said, "Tea endows one with vitality of body, peace of mind, and clarity of purpose when taken over a long period of time."

Lore and legends concerning the origin of tea are plentiful, colored and flavored with cultural myths and religious symbolism from era to era. Here is one such legend: In A.D. 520 an Indian monk—Bodhidharma—came to China. Bodhidharma, Ta-Mo in Chinese, was the founder of the Zen sect of Buddhism that taught meditation. Soon after arriving in China, he demonstrated meditation by sitting in front of a cave wall for nine years. Once he was so angry with himself for falling asleep during meditation that he cut off his eyelids and threw them on the ground. From the spot where his eyelids touched the earth grew the first tea plant, to help keep man from sleep.

Tea is the drink of China. There are mild teas of golden color, fragrant flower-scented teas, smoky red teas, pungent, haunting tea, and medicinal tea, a thick muddy horror. We drink them all.

We were taught as children that tea's nature is cool, quiet and calm, that it endows one with ethereal purity, expands one's spirit, clears one's mind and leads one toward quiet contemplation and self-realization.

Tea has often been associated with Taoist monks, the nature-oriented recluses who drink tea deep in the mountains, under the pines near a stream, in a flowing robe, away from the foolish ambitions of the vulgar world, its glory and wealth.

Some ancient tea masters and connoisseurs admonished us not to contaminate tea with food, noise or worldly people: one should not gulp tea but sip it moderately. One should not drink tea unless one prepares it oneself, using only the proper tools, just the right fire, only the purest water, roasting it, grinding it, brewing it to perfection. Only then may one properly drink tea.

Modern tea connoisseurs repeat these admonitions with sternness and blind devotion, saying nothing about the pleasure of drinking tea without pretention, in a common atmosphere, among ordinary people. We may gulp tea by the gallon when thirsty; or drink it with oily food to help digestion. Sometimes we prefer to drink it with loud-voiced company, in a noisy restaurant, talking all at the same time. Occasionally, we enjoy tea in solitude, listening to the chirping of birds or watching the drifting snow, in quiet happiness; or share it with someone who knows our heart, in leisure and with few words. Also, there are times we need tea to quench our trifling worries or worldly desires, and allow us to let things be.

And in my family we drank tea because my father denounced water for being tasteless, soft drinks for dulling his tongue; milk was pronounced fit only for babies or for those with tuberculosis; wine, he declared, made him foolish. And so we drank tea.

How to Make Chinese Tea

There is no exact way of making Chinese tea, because each tea's nature is different. In general, green tea retains its natural purest flavor; therefore a smaller amount should be used—otherwise the infusion comes out tasting bitter.

Use a slightly larger amount of red or semi-red tea to bring out its full aroma and taste. The following steps are just a guideline. The way to make a good cup of tea is to learn the character of each tea, trying it until you succeed.

1. Use a clean china teapot. (Tea disagrees chemically with a metal teapot.)

2. Scald the teapot's interior with boiling water and discard the water. Add tea leaves. Use about one teaspoonful of tea leaves for each cup. (A Chinese teacup holds about ⅓ of a measuring cup.)

3. Pour in boiling water. The water should come to a full boil, then immediately be added to the tea leaves.

4. Cover to steep. After about 3 minutes, the tea is ready for drinking. It may be reinfused two more times without adding more tea leaves.

Varieties of Chinese Teas

Tea grows mostly in the south and southwest part of China and in Taiwan. There are uncountable varieties. Of the following kinds of tea, many are available in the States, but some of them can be found only in tea shops in the Orient. Here is a sample selection. *(Note: The Chinese refer to black tea as red tea.)*

Teas from Kwangtung Province

Sui Hsien Tea (Water Nymph Tea)—green tea
Sao May Tea (Eyebrows of Longevity Tea)—green tea
Oolong Tea (Black Dragon Tea)—semi-red tea
Ching Yun Tea (Clear Distance Tea)—red tea
Loong So Tea (Dragon Beard Tea)—green tea
Lychee Tea—red tea

Tea from Kwangsi Province

Cassia Tea—semi-red tea

Tea from Yunnan Province

    Pu-Erh Tea (or Po Nay Tea)—semi-red tea

Tea from Fukien Province

    Tikuanyin Tea (Iron Goddess Tea)—semi-red tea

Teas from Chinkiang Province

    Loong Jan Tea (Dragon Well Tea)—green tea
    Fragrant Petals Tea—green tea

Tea from Taiwan

    Tung Ting Oolong Tea (Black Dragon Tea)—semi-red tea

Teas for Every Taste

Lychee Tea: It has a natural sweet taste, full and fragrant.

Jasmine Tea: It has a flowery aroma, is gentle and soothing.

Tikuanyin Tea: Its flavor is musty, slightly smoky, and full of body.

Chrysanthemum Tea: It is a golden color, mildly fragrant, and is the only Chinese tea drunk with rock sugar.

Teas Popular Among Chinese

Pu-Erh Tea: It tastes herbal and slightly musty. The flavor bears the strength of its mountain and earth.

Loong Jan Tea: It gives a light, greenish infusion, and its taste is fresh and pure.

Sui Hsien Tea: Its flavor is mild, smooth, and gently scented.

Sao May Tea: It has the pure, natural clear flavor of a green tea; it is light and refreshing.

Tung Ting Oolong Tea: This is a very famous tea of Taiwan. Its flavor is full, aromatic, and vigorous.

chinese cooking utensils
and cooking methods

What Kind of Wok Do You Need?

Woks come in various sizes and metals. The most suitable wok is carbon steel, 14 or 16 inches in diameter with either two earlike handles or a long wooden handle. Besides the wok itself, a matching lid is essential for steaming, smoking, poaching, and roasting. The ideal lid is a tall and roomy one made of aluminum, so that it will not rust and is able to cover a large chicken as well as allow steam or smoke to circulate inside. A collar is also needed to steady the wok. I prefer one that has round edges rather than the sharp zigzag edges that often scratch the stove.

Woks made with stainless steel or aluminum are free from rust, but cannot be used for smoking chicken (recipe in my first book, *The Classic Chinese Cookbook,* Harper & Row, 1976).

The various kinds of electric woks available in the States are not yet perfect for Chinese cooking. The lid is always too low and small, unable to cover a large chicken. Also, the wok has a built-in heating unit, which is a handicap in stir-fry cooking. For instance, when the heat is too high, the cook can't remove the wok to adjust the heat, which is crucial in the fast action of stir-fry cooking.

Now, there is a wok made especially for electric stoves. It is made of carbon steel and has sloping sides like a regular wok, but has a flat bottom to sit directly on a burner; thus the food in the wok is heated much faster than with a regular one.

How to Treat and Care for a Carbon Steel Wok: If a wok is new, clean it thoroughly with mild detergent, dry it, then wipe the inside with a paper towel slightly dampened with vegetable oil. After the cooking is done, immediately soak the wok in hot water so that food sticking to it comes off easily. Wash it with mild detergent and always dry it thoroughly over medium heat as soon as it is washed. If it looks dull (especially after it is used for steaming), wipe it with a little oil. *Never* wash a wok in a dishwasher. Also, do not store it in humid places such as a damp basement unless it is well coated with oil.

Cooking on Electric Stoves

If you have a gas stove, it is a blessing for Chinese cooking, because the heat can be adjusted easily. However, if you have an electric stove do not be discouraged. Either buy a wok made for electric stoves or follow these directions:

For Stir-Frying: Turn on two burners, one high temperature and the other low, so that you can adjust the temperature by switching the wok to the heat you wish at that moment. Also, if you want to heat the wok fast, put it directly on the range without the collar, and use one hand to steady it while cooking.

For Deep-Frying: It takes a long time to heat a wok full of oil to deep-fry temperature if it sits on a collar; but without a collar for steadiness, it is much too hazardous. If you have an electric stove, I suggest that you use a pot or a deep-fryer for deep-frying.

Steamers and Steaming Methods

Steaming food is very popular among the Chinese. For steaming not only uses less oil, saves fuel, space, time, and work, but also makes food taste good. Therefore, a steamed dish is usually included in a Chinese family meal.

A Chinese meal always consists of a few dishes, not one main course; but each dish is a main course, equally important as the others. In Chinese restaurants or at banquets dishes are served one at a time, whereas in a family meal all dishes are served at the same time. Therefore, a Chinese cook will plan a menu that can be cooked and served without effort. It is wise not to stir-fry or pan-fry all the dishes just before serving, unless the cook does not wish to sit down to eat with the family.

A resourceful cook will plan at least a dish or two that demands less attention and effort or can be prepared in advance. Steaming food is as simple as putting food in an oven; one just leaves it until the bell rings. A few different dishes can be steamed at the same time, each dish in its own steamer basket, stacked one on top of the other.

There are various ways of steaming food. Some food is put directly on a steamer basket or a perforated tray to drain off juice or liquid that would make it soggy. Other foods are placed on a heatproof plate to collect the juice while steaming. Also, there are dishes that can be steamed without a steamer or a perforated tray, but put directly over rice as the rice is being cooked.

Steaming in the Bamboo Steamer

Bamboo steamers vary from tiny 4-inch dim sum steamers to 16-inch seafood or poultry steamers. Each steamer set consists of at least one round basket with a solidly woven lid on top. The most practical size is a 12- or 14-inch one in which you can steam a wide range of food.

Put the food (chiaotses, buns, poultry, meat, rice, etc.) in the steamer basket. To steam rice, line the basket with cheesecloth so that the rice will not fall through. If you have a large amount and more than one steamer basket, you may place food in all the baskets, stack them, and cover with a lid.

Use a wok that is about 1 to 2 inches larger than the steamer; pour in enough water to reach at least 3 inches below the steamer. Bring the water to a rolling boil; place steamer basket(s) over the water, and steam over high heat according to the time given in the recipe.

How to Care for a Bamboo Steamer: After each use, wash basket(s) and lid with mild detergent; brush out food particles; shake off water and air dry.

Steaming in a Metal Steamer

Aluminum or stainless steel steamers are popularly used in restaurants and at home, because they last longer and are easy to clean. Each steamer set includes a lid, metal perforated basket(s), and a tightly fitted steamer pot to hold water for steaming rather than a wok.

Pour in enough water to reach about a third of the way up the pot. Bring water to a full boil. Put perforated basket(s) containing food in pot over water; cover with lid; and steam over high heat according to the time given in the recipe.

Steaming with a Perforated Tray or a Wire Rack

If you do not have a set of bamboo or metal steamers, you can substitute a round metal perforated tray or a wire rack (a round cake rack will do). However, the perforated tray or rack should be just slightly smaller than the wok, so that it sits high in the wok and far above the water to avoid flooding. Perforated trays ranging from 10 to 14 inches are available in Chinese hardware stores, Chinese markets, and cooking utensil stores.

Steaming in a Regular Pot

For steaming a small amount of food (sausages, leftovers, steamed buns, etc.), if you do not want to use a wok, steamer, tray, or rack mentioned above, use a regular pot with a tight lid. Buy a small steaming stand with high legs in Chinatown or make one with wire to fit in a 3- or 4-quart pot. Put the food in a heatproof bowl or on a plate, then place it on the steaming stand over boiling water. Cover and steam according to the time given in the recipe.

Rules for Steaming

1. There should be enough water in the wok or pot to create steam and last through the steaming.

2. Never start steaming food before the water is boiling rapidly.

3. If the steaming time is long, do not allow water to evaporate; add boiling water to maintain the water level as it is needed.

4. Do not peek while the food is steaming: control your concern and curiosity. Permit the steam to do its magic. Peeking not only lets the vital steam escape and stops the steaming process, but also will ruin some dishes that require the powerful constant heat.

Chinese Clay Pots

The Chinese believe that whatever is cooked in a clay pot tastes better than it does cooked in metal. These ancient cooking vessels are now available in Chinese markets in the States; the inside is fired with a dark-brown glaze which is free of odor and also makes the pot very easy to clean.

Some clay pots are supported by iron wire to help to distribute heat evenly. All of them are made to be used on the wood or charcoal stoves of China, but are also safe on gas stoves and in ovens. However, it is a risk to use them on electric stoves—the heat is too direct and intense.

All-Purpose Clay Pot: This clay pot is endlessly useful; sizes vary from 1 to 5 quarts. Its rustic charm makes an attractive presentation from stove or oven to the table.

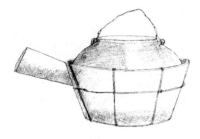

Cow's Head Clay Pot: This pot is tall and has a narrow mouth. A large pot is more useful than a small one. It's used mainly for cooking soup, congee, and a traditional dish named "childbirth ginger," to nourish women after giving birth.

How to Cure a Chinese Clay Pot: Before using a new clay pot, it should be immersed in water and soaked overnight. Then fill the wet soaked pot with water and bring it to a boil over medium heat. Pour off the water, and the pot is cured, ready to be used for cooking.

Do not heat a clay pot without oil or water in it. Also, moderate heat is recommended if the pot is half full or less. All clay pots are dishwasher safe.

Deep-Fry Drainer and Its Use

Two kinds of Chinese drainers are available in the States. One is made of shiny brass wires woven by hand and connected to a bamboo handle. The other is made of stainless steel with a perforated bowl. The sizes vary from 4 to 8 inches. For family cooking, a 6-inch one is more useful.

The drainer is used for scooping out and draining fried food, blanched meat, vegetables, and noodles. Either kind is dishwasher safe.

Chinese Cleaver and Its Use

Chinese cleavers come in different weights and are used for different purposes. The cleaver blade is about 8 inches long and 3 to 4 inches wide. The thick, heavy cleaver is for cutting meat with bones in it, and is called a "bone cleaver." Thinner and lighter cleavers are used for slicing meat and cutting vegetables.

Use each kind of cleaver for its particular function. If you use a meat slicing cleaver to chop bones, you will destroy its edges. And the heavy cleaver is awkward and tiring to use for slicing meat and vegetables.

In addition to cutting purposes, a cleaver can also be used to slide under food and carry it from the chopping board to other places. You may also place cloves of garlic on a hard surface and whack them with the flat of the cleaver blade; the garlic skins will come off with the slightest pull.

Stir-Frying

The Chinese call stir-frying *chow,* meaning turning and stirring food quickly in hot oil over high heat. A dish takes only a few minutes to finish.

The most important and basic element of stir-frying is to heat the wok hot *before* adding oil. And the oil should be *hot* before adding the ingredients, for heat releases their pleasing aroma and draws out their full flavor. If you miss this basic step, you fail as a Chinese cook before you start.

It is important to stir and turn the food constantly and quickly with a spatula, so that it will not be burned or stick to the wok. Also, have all ingredients cut and the sauces prepared. Put them within reach to avoid dashing about to search for ingredients while stir-frying.

Deep-Frying

For deep-frying, it is very important to have the oil at the right temperature (375 degrees). If the oil is not hot enough, residue from meat and poultry and seafood will cloud it. Also, the food will absorb more oil and thus become soggy and greasy. However, if it is too hot, the food will burn or get brown outside in a second and not be cooked inside.

The Chinese do not use a cooking thermometer, but judge the oil by experienced eyes, or test it by dipping a dry bamboo or wood chopstick into the hot oil. If a great many sizzling bubbles quickly gather around the chopstick, the oil is ready for deep-frying. If the bubbles surround the chopstick slowly, the oil is not quite ready. Be sure that the chopstick is dry. A wet chopstick does not work. If the oil is smoking, do not put in anything. Turn off the heat and let it cool. Overheated oil is flammable, so do not allow a wokful of oil to become smoking hot.

Never let water drop in hot oil! Not only do oil and water refuse to mix in harmony—they quarrel noisily and sometimes even fire shots at you for putting them together. So be sure to dry food thoroughly before slipping it into the oil.

Now you can buy a round screen with a handle in dime stores or hardware stores to cover the oil to avoid splattering while deep-frying.

Oil left over from deep-frying can be recycled (see page 207).

Blanching Food in Oil

This method is called *yo-pao,* and is used mostly by Chinese chefs. The purpose is to achieve the maximum tenderness, smoothness, and lightness of the food. It is different from deep-frying. The food is not fried to golden brown, but is removed from the oil immediately when its color changes and it is just done. Usually the food is shredded or sliced into thin pieces before blanching.

For meat: Heat the amount of oil required in recipe over medium heat to deep-fry temperature (about 375 degrees), or test with a chopstick (as explained under Deep-Frying). Add the meat and quickly stir to separate the pieces. As soon as the meat loses its redness (it takes less than a minute), remove it with a Chinese drainer or a large slotted spoon.

For poultry or seafood: Heat oil (amount required in recipe) over medium heat to moderate temperature (about 300 degrees), or test it with a piece of scallion; it should just sizzle but not spin around. Add poultry or seafood and quickly stir to separate pieces. In less than a minute, the ingredients should turn a milky-white or pink. Remove with a Chinese drainer or a large slotted spoon.

The oil left over from blanching can be reused (see page 207).

Blanching Food in Water

Chicken and vegetables are blanched briefly in boiling water to attain the maximum smoothness of the chicken and the brightest green color of the vegetables. But this method does not work with red meat such as beef.

For chicken: Use 1 quart of boiling water for each cup of shredded, sliced, or diced raw chicken. Before blanching, the chicken has to be combined with egg white, cornstarch, and other ingredients according to the recipe. Immerse chicken in boiling water and turn off heat at once. Stir to separate pieces. Allow chicken to blanch in water for 1 minute. Pour into a colander. Rinse thoroughly in running cold water to prevent further cooking. Drain, and use as required in recipe.

For vegetables: Use 2 quarts of boiling water for each half pound of fresh vegetables. Immerse vegetables in boiling water, turn off heat, pour into a colander, and rinse thoroughly in running cold water to prevent further cooking. Use as required in recipe.

CHINESE COOKING INGREDIENTS

Abalone (Canned)

The canned variety usually comes from Japan or Mexico. It is already cooked and ready to be served. Some brands are very delicious and quite expensive. Cooking time should be short; excessive heat will toughen the abalone and make it chewy and rubbery. The liquid from the can is good for soup and congee.

Storing: Drain and rinse. Store in a covered jar with enough fresh cold water to cover it. Refrigerate it and change the water every other day. It will keep for about 2 weeks.

Agar-Agar (Tai Choy)

A dried seaweed with no flavor, agar-agar is sold in packages, and comes mostly from Japan. It resembles a cross between thin rice sticks and bean thread noodles, and functions like unflavored gelatin in making sweet dishes. Cook it in water until it is dissolved, and chill. For use in salad dishes, soak agar-agar in cold water and cut into 1½-inch lengths.

Soaking: For cold dishes only; soak in cold water for about 30 minutes or until soft. Drain and cut into 1½-inch lengths with scissors. Then tear them into shreds like noodles.

Storing: Agar-agar needs no refrigeration. It will keep forever.

Anise (Star)

A reddish brown, hard, dried Chinese spice that looks like a half-inch eight-pointed star and smells like licorice. Star anise is used to flavor meat and poultry. It is sold in packages (usually with the points apart) and available in Chinese food stores.

Storing: Stored in a covered jar, it will keep forever.

Bamboo Leaves (Dried)

Dried bamboo leaves are about 16 inches long and 3 to 4 inches wide. They come from the subtropical parts of China, and are used to wrap food and impart a subtle flavor. Sold in bundles in Chinese grocery stores.

Storing: Will keep indefinitely.

Bamboo Shoots

Young shoots of tropical bamboo, they are the color of ivory and delicious when young and fresh. In the States, bamboo shoots are usually imported in cans.

The canned variety is canned in plain water in chunks or in slices. Rinse in fresh cold water to get rid of the sour odor before using.

Storing: Refrigerate in a covered jar with enough water to cover them; change water every other day. They will keep for a few weeks.

Bean Curd (Five-Fragrance)

Slightly smaller than ordinary bean curd, this is flat and square, about 2 by 2 inches, hard and dark brown in color and seasoned with five-fragrance powder. It is available in Chinese grocery stores.

Storing: Store in refrigerator. Will keep about a week.

Bean Curd (Fresh)

These little squares are made of pressed puréed soybeans. Bean curd is smooth, soft, and custardlike. It usually comes in a 3- or 4-inch-square, 1-inch-thick, bricklike cake. It is white in color and bland in taste, but quick to absorb the flavor of the other ingredients with which it is cooked. It is inexpensive and high in protein. Although used as a vegetable, it serves the purpose of "meat" and "milk" for the Chinese. Buy the soft variety for preparing soup, and the hard kind for stuffed bean curd dishes or for frying.

Storing: Store like bamboo shoots, but change water daily; will keep for a week or more.

Bean Curd Skins

These shiny, brownish yellow, paper-thin skins are dried but flexible. Some are 24 inches in diameter. They are the rich cream which floats on top of the soy bean milk, and are mostly used as pastry skins. They are sold in packages in Chinese food stores.

Storing: Refrigerate in plastic bag. Will keep for a week or two.

Bean Curd Cheese (Red)

Labeled as red bean curd, this is a brick-red 2-inch square, about 1 inch thick, fermented with red rice, salt, water, and rice wine. Pungent and salty in taste, it is mostly used as a seasoning in cooking. It is sold in cans or jars in Chinese food stores.

Storing: Refrigerate in glass jar; will keep for months.

Bean Curd Puffs (Fried)

These cushionlike cakes sold individually are golden, fluffy, and spongy. They are available in Chinese and Japanese food stores.

Storing: Refrigerate in a plastic bag. They will keep for about two weeks. They can also be frozen and will keep for several months.

Bean Paste (Sweet Red)

This paste made by puréeing Chinese red beans, sugar, and shortening is dark-red in color, thick and quite sweet. Used in sweet pastries and sweet dishes, it is sold in cans in Chinese and Japanese food stores, or by weight in Chinese pastry stores.

Storing: Will keep for weeks if refrigerated in a covered jar.

Bean Sprouts (Fresh)

These tiny sprouts (also called green or mung bean sprouts) have white bodies, yellow heads, green hoods, and small tails. The green hoods should be removed when washing. The Chinese spend hours leisurely pinching off the tails, too, so that the sprouts will look neater.

They are delicate, crunchy, and very inexpensive. Cooking time should be short, as prolonged cooking will ruin their crunchiness.

Fresh bean sprouts are available in Chinese or Japanese food stores and some supermarkets. If they look slightly brownish, they are not fresh and are turning sour. Try another store. And never, never use canned bean sprouts.

Storing: Rinse well in cold water. Refrigerate in a container with fresh water. Change the water daily and they will keep for about a week.

Bean Sauces

Ground Bean Sauce

This brown, thick, pungent purée sauce is made from yellow soybeans, flour, salt, and water. It is sold in cans in Oriental food stores.

Storing: Refrigerate in a covered jar, and it will keep for months.

Szechwan Sweet Bean Sauce

Sometimes this sauce is labeled sweet bean paste. It is not sweet! It is very salty and pungent, and tastes very much like ground bean sauce. Called for in many Szechwan dishes, it can be used interchangeably with ground bean sauce. It is available in 6-ounce cans in Chinese food stores.

Storing: Refrigerate in a covered jar; it will keep for months.

Szechwan Hot (Chili) Bean Sauce

Used in Szechwan dishes, this sauce is orange-brown in color, very salty, pungent, spicy, and hot. It is available in 6-ounce cans in Chinese food stores.

Storing: Store as you would Szechwan sweet bean sauce.

Black Beans (Salted)

Black beans preserved in ginger, garlic, and (of course) salt are used as a seasoning in food. Before cooking, they are strong, pungent, and very salty in taste. Rinse them in hot water before using. After being cooked, they give a delicious flavor to food. Black beans are sold in cans or in bags in Chinese food stores and gourmet food stores.

Storing: Keep in covered jar; no refrigeration is needed; will keep for months.

Bok Choy (Fresh)

"White vegetable" in English, bok choy is a delicious leafy plant with long white stalks and large ruffled green leaves. It is sold fresh by weight in Chinese food stores and in some supermarkets.

Storing: Will keep about 5 days in refrigerator.

Chinese Celery Cabbage

Shaped like a short, stout celery, celery cabbage (also called Tientsin cabbage) has wide, yellow-white, tightly packed stalks, 9 to 10 inches in length. It is crisp and mild in taste and can be eaten raw. Chinese grocery stores and many supermarkets sell it.

Storing: Wrap and refrigerate; will keep for 2 weeks or more.

Snow Cabbage

Also called red-in-snow cabbage, this is canned chopped pickled cabbage. Salty and tasty, it is used in stir-fried dishes and in soup. Since many different kinds of cabbage are labeled in English "Pickled Chinese Cabbage," shop at a Chinese grocery store and take along the Shopping List at the end of this book.

Storing: Keep refrigerated; it will keep in a covered jar for weeks.

Chicken Broth (Clear)

If you prefer, make your own chicken broth. But many Chinese like College Inn chicken broth, which is stacked up in most Chinese grocery stores. This canned broth is clear and tasty. Use it straight or mix it with water.

Chili Oil
(see Sauces and Dips)

Chili Peppers (Dried)

These orange-red dried hot peppers are the size of a small finger. Use them with the seeds which are essential for the hotness. Buy them in Chinese and Italian grocery stores or substitute the crushed hot peppers sold in supermarkets.

Storing: Stored in a covered jar, they will keep for months.

Chili Sauce (Chinese)

This chili sauce is available in Chinese grocery stores. It is made with chili, vinegar, salt and starch. Thicker than Tabasco sauce but milder and less vinegary, it is used only as a condiment and may be replaced by Tabasco sauce.

Storing: Will keep for months in refrigerator.

Cloud Ears

These black, small, crinkled dried tree fungi (also known as tree mushrooms) resemble a cluster of ear-shaped clouds. They are soft and resilient in texture, subtle and dainty in taste. Soak them before you use them; they will expand two to three times beyond their original size.

Storing: Will keep indefinitely in a covered jar.

Coriander (Fresh)

A very pungent herb with delicate leaves, coriander is good for both seasoning and garnishing. It is also known as cilantro or Spanish parsley or dhania. You can buy it in Chinese, Spanish or Indian grocery stores (and it's easy to grow from seed).

Storing: Remove yellowing leaves and store in a jar with water for the roots and a plastic bag to cover the leaves. It should keep at least a week in the refrigerator.

Coconut Milk (Unsweetened)

It is also called coconut cream. Thick cream extracted from fresh coconut meat, it is imported from the Philippines and available in Chinese grocery stores.

Storing: Leftovers can be frozen; will keep for months.

Curry Paste

Curry paste is pungent and spicy, with much more strength and aroma then curry powder. It is sold in Chinese grocery stores. Buy the brands that are made in India or bottled in India for an American company.

Storing: Refrigerate in jar; will keep for months.

Duck Eggs (Salted)

Duck or large chicken eggs steeped in salted water for about a month. They are available in Chinese grocery stores. If you wish to make your own, dissolve 1 cup of salt in 6 cups water plus ½ cup of sherry, then add 12 eggs, cover and let stand for a month, drain. These will keep for weeks in the refrigerator.

Five-Fragrance Powder

A mixture of five ground spices (star anise, cloves, fennel, cinnamon, and peppercorns), this is cinnamon colored and fragrant. Use it sparingly. It is sold in packages in Oriental grocery stores.

Storing: Will keep indefinitely in a covered jar.

Flower Peppercorns

Also called Szechwan peppercorns or wild peppercorns, these are reddish brown, gentle and delicate in their hotness and scent. They are sold in packages in Chinese food stores.

Storing: Will keep indefinitely in a covered jar.

Flower Peppercorn Powder
(See Sauces and Dips)

Garlic

Do not substitute garlic powder. The best way to peel the garlic skin is to give the clove a quick smack with the flat side of a cleaver. The skin will be easily removed with just a gentle pull. Never burn garlic while cooking. Burned garlic not only loses its flavor but adds a bitter taste.

Ginger Root (Fresh)

A very important seasoning in Chinese cooking, especially in cooking seafood, ginger root eliminates fishy and gamy odors and adds a zesty flavor. It comes in a variety of shapes, like a thick potato grown with knobs. When it is young, the skin is smooth and has the color of a young potato; darker skin indicates an older root which is dry and fibrous. The meat is ivory in color, and has a clean fresh smell as well as a hot spicy taste. Never substitute ginger powder or dried ginger!

Storing: Wrap in plastic wrap and keep it at room temperature; it will keep many weeks. Do not refrigerate it; it will turn a bluish color and become moldy. It can also be sliced and frozen, but use it in cooking without thawing. It becomes spongy if it is thawed.

Ginger Juice

Ginger juice is not available in Chinese grocery stores. The easiest way to make it is to press a small chunk of fresh ginger root with a garlic press. Catch the juice in a small bowl. If you do not have a garlic press, just mince the ginger finely.

Ham (Chinese and Smithfield)

Chinese ham tastes like Smithfield ham, which is cured and smoked in Smithfield, Virginia. It is salty and very tasty. You can buy it in Chinese grocery stores or gourmet stores.

Storing: Wrap and refrigerate. It will keep for weeks and can also be frozen.

Hoisin Sauce

Hoisin means seafood in Chinese. It is a thick brownish red paste: spicy, salty, and moderately sweet. The ingredients are water, garlic, chili, flour, and spices. Used in cooking and as a condiment, it is sold in Oriental food stores and gourmet food stores in cans or in bottles.

Storing: Will keep for weeks in covered jar.

Jellyfish Skin

A sea organism, dried, salted and pressed. It has little flavor, but is crunchy and resilient. It must be rinsed and soaked before use. It is sold in Chinese grocery stores.

Storing: Will keep for months in refrigerator if salt is not removed.

Lemon Sauce

This sauce, made from lemon, sugar and water, is thick like jam. It is sweet, lemony but gently bitter and is used as a table condiment and for cooking. Bottled in Hong Kong or in China, it is available in Chinese grocery stores.

Storing: Will keep for months in refrigerator.

Lily Buds (Dried)

Lily buds are also known as golden needles. The better kinds are still flexible, not brittle, and are a pale gold color. They are sold in packages in Chinese grocery stores.

Storing: Will keep indefinitely in covered jar.

Lotus Leaves

The leaves, fresh or dried, are primarily used to wrap and give a subtle flavor to food. They are available dried in some Chinese grocery stores.

Lotus Seeds (Dried)

Lotus seeds, which represent fertility and birth, are used in many dishes. They are sold in Chinese grocery stores.

Storing: Will keep indefinitely in a covered jar.

Mushrooms

Chinese Dried Mushrooms

Also known as black mushrooms, these dried mushrooms are black, aromatic, and luscious. Their size ranges from ½ inch to 2½ inches in diameter. They are used in innumerable ways, and sold in Chinese grocery stores and gourmet food stores.

Storing: Will keep for months in a tightly covered container.

Golden Mushrooms (Canned)

These mushrooms have long stems and tiny caps; golden in color, they resemble long nails. They are canned in salted water, and have lost much of their woody flavor. Rinse them in cold water before use. They are available in Chinese grocery stores.

Storing: Place in a jar, cover with water, and refrigerate. Change water every other day. They will keep for a few weeks.

Straw Mushrooms (Canned)

They are also called grass mushrooms. They are canned in water and sold in Chinese grocery stores. Rinse them before using.

Storing: Store in a covered jar with enough water to cover them. Refrigerate; change water every other day; will keep for a few weeks.

Mustard Greens (Pickled)

Also labeled as salted mustard greens, these are sold in barrels or in cans in Chinese grocery stores.

Storing: Will keep for a few days in refrigerator or for months in the freezer.

Mustard Pickle (Szechwan)

Sometimes this pickle is labeled Szechwan cabbage, Szechwan jah choy, or Szechwan vegetable. It comes in chunks in cans and is sold in Chinese food stores. It is hot, spicy, and salty, and must be rinsed before cooking.

Storing: Do not rinse off salt and spices. Put in a tightly covered jar. This will keep for months in the refrigerator and also can be frozen.

Noodles

Fresh Noodles
(See pages 138–142)

Bean Thread Noodles

Also known as peastarch noodles or cellophane noodles, these are wiry, hard, clear white noodles made from mung peas. If used in soup, they must be soaked until soft and translucent. They should not be overcooked, as prolonged cooking will make them mushy.

It is not necessary to presoak them if they are deep-fried. They pop up from the oil like a snow-white nest. Sold in 2- to 6-ounce packages.

Storing: Will keep indefinitely without refrigeration.

Sah Ho Rice Noodles
(See page 164)

Storing: Refrigerate in a plastic bag; they will keep for about 5 days.

Dried Rice Noodles

Also labeled "dried rice sticks," they look almost like bean thread noodles, but are whiter and more brittle. Use them in stir-frying, soup, or deep-frying. For soup or stir-frying, they must be presoaked in hot tap water for about 15 minutes or until soft. There is no need to soak them if they are deep-fried. They pop up from the hot oil in a white nest. Buy them in packages in Chinese grocery stores.

Storing: Will keep indefinitely without refrigeration.

Oils

Peanut Oil, Corn Oil, and Vegetable Oil

We Chinese prefer to use peanut oil in the Orient, but I find corn oil is very good in the States. So use either peanut or corn oil for stir-fry cooking. For deep-frying, corn oil is the best choice, but vegetable oil will do, and it is more economical.

Storing:
- Oil can be reused many times. Strain it and keep it refrigerated. Discard the oil when it becomes dark and heavy with residues.
- Oil used for cooking fish should be kept in a separate bottle. Reuse it for fish only. Keep refrigerated.
- To remove odor from oil: Heat the used oil to deep-fry temperature (375 degrees). Add 2 to 3 slices of fresh ginger root or raw peeled potato; fry until they turn golden. Then discard them; the oil will be refreshed.

Chili Oil
(See Sauces and Dips)

Sesame Oil

This savory, aromatic, topaz-colored oil, made from roasted white sesame seeds, is used sparingly to flavor food. The pale sesame seed oil sold in some health food stores is not the same, and has no place in Chinese cooking. Sesame oil is available in Oriental food stores.

Storing: Will keep for months in refrigerator.

Oyster Sauce

Labeled "oyster-flavored sauce," this thick caramel-colored sauce is made from oyster extraction, water, salt, and starch. It is pungent, salty, and tasty. There are many grades; the best kind is thinner and more runny; the inferior sauce is usually too thick to pour and sometimes foamy. Oyster sauce is sold in Chinese grocery stores.

Storing: Covered and refrigerated, the sauce will keep for months.

Peanut Butter and Sesame Paste

In China, roasted peanuts are eaten as snacks, as popular as potato chips in the States. Peanut butter and sesame seed paste are used interchangeably in cooking.

Sesame seed paste is made from roasted sesame seeds and oil; it has a very slightly bitter taste. Make your own sesame paste (page 208) or use peanut butter.

Storing: Keep sesame paste as you would peanut butter.

Plum Sauce

Plum sauce is also known as duck sauce; it's a thick chutney-like sauce that's spicy, sweet, and sour, made from plums, ginger, apricots, chili, vinegar, sugar, and water. It is used as a table condiment and in cooking. If it is used as a dip, it must be diluted (see Sauces and Dips). It is sold in Chinese food stores and gourmet shops.

Storing: Will keep for months if refrigerated in a covered jar.

Red Dates (Dried)

These Chinese red dates are used to sweeten soup or in pastry. You can buy them in Chinese grocery stores.

Storing: Will keep for months in a covered jar.

Rice (Glutinous)

Also known as sweet rice, glutinous rice is short, plump, milk-white, and pearly. It turns sticky and glutinous when cooked and is used in making dumplings, pastries, puddings, and stuffings. It is sold in Oriental food stores.

Storing: Will keep indefinitely in a tightly covered jar.

Rice Powder

This powder is ground from ordinary rice. It is sold in Chinese grocery stores.

Storing: Store as flour.

Rice Powder (Glutinous)

This fine powder, ground from glutinous rice, is whiter than wheat flour. It becomes sticky, soft, and chewy when it is cooked. It is used in making dumplings, sweet dishes, and pastries. You can buy it in Oriental food stores.

Storing: Store as flour.

Sah Goh

Sah goh means "sandy tuber" in Chinese, for it grows in sandy soil. It is also called *jicama* in Spanish. It is shaped like an onion, but has tough tan skin. The flesh is like that of water chestnuts, mildly sweet, and stays crisp when heated. The Chinese eat it raw or use it in stir-frying. It is available in summer months in Chinese and Spanish stores.

Storing: Keep in refrigerator; use in one week.

Saté Sauce
(See page 156)

Sausages (Chinese Duck Liver)

Duck livers are cured with seasoning and fat pork, then forced into casings which are tied in pairs to air-dry. They are black and white, and rich and pungent after they are steamed. They are sold in Chinese grocery stores.

Storing: Store as Chinese pork sausages.

Sausages (Chinese Pork)

Minced pork is cured with seasonings, then forced into casings and tied in pairs to air-dry. Each link is about 5 to 6 inches long, and ½ inch in diameter. Dark red and white in color, these sausages are savory and rich in taste. They are sold by weight in Chinese grocery stores.

Storing: Wrap and refrigerate or hang in cool place; will keep for weeks. Will also freeze well.

Shao Mai Skins
(See page 13)

Shrimp (Dried)

Shelled uncooked shrimp dried in the sun, these have a sharp flavor and are used in small amounts for stuffing or soup. They must be soaked before using. The best kind are orange-pink, about an inch long. If their color is dark and the shrimp becomes powdery, they are no longer good. Buy them in Chinese grocery stores.

Storing: Will keep for months in a tightly covered jar.

Shrimp Chips

These thin, hard, quarter-sized chips come in assorted pastel colors. When deep-fried, they puff up and double in size. Tasty and crisp, they can be eaten as a snack like potato chips or used as a garnish. They are sold in Oriental food shops.

Storing: Will keep indefinitely in a covered jar.

Snow Peas (Fresh)

The Chinese also call them Holland peas; they supposedly originated in Holland. Flat and light green in color, they are crisp and gently sweet if they are not overcooked. Eat pods and all. Use frozen ones only as a last resort.

Storing: Keep in refrigerator; use within a week.

Soy Sauces

Soy sauces are the most important seasoning in Chinese cooking. There are many varieties and grades. Thin or black, good or bad, domestic or imported, all are labeled "soy sauce" in English. Knowing their differences and using the right kind is the key to authentic, good-tasting dishes. The basic and frequently used soy sauces are black soy sauce and thin soy sauce. Others, such as fish-flavored soy, mushroom soy, and double black soy, are regional soy sauces for certain local dishes.

Black Soy Sauce

This is also known as dark soy sauce. It is made from soybeans, caramel, sugar, flour, salt, and water. Darker and heavier than thin soy sauce, it has a salty but slightly sweet taste. If you cannot read Chinese and don't know whether the bottle is black soy sauce or thin soy sauce, read the ingredients. If the ingredients contain sugar and caramel, it is black soy sauce; without them it is thin soy sauce. For stir-frying I prefer the black soy sauce made by Amoy Canning Company. Soy sauce labeled "double dark soy sauce" is good for red cooking but not as good for stir-frying: it is too heavy and sometimes too salty. For good and authentic flavor, do not substitute American-made soy sauce.

Storing: If it is not used very often, keep it in the refrigerator, and it will keep for months. If a white substance appears on the surface, the soy has turned bad; discard it.

Double Black Soy Sauce

Double black soy sauce, darker and heavier in taste than black soy sauce, is used in red cooking to add color and strength. The taste varies with the company that produces it. Some are slightly sweeter or saltier than others. I prefer the double black soy sauce made by Yuet Heung Yuen Company from Hong Kong. It is available in Chinese grocery stores.

Storing: Store as black soy sauce.

Fish-Flavored Soy Sauce

Fish-flavored soy is a southern soy, made with salt, water, and extract of fish. Its color is slightly lighter than the thin soy sauce. Use it as a dip or in dishes that require a fish flavor. It is available in Chinese grocery stores.

Storing: Store as black soy sauce.

Mushroom Soy Sauce

Mushroom soy is very much like black soy sauce, but richer in taste and in color; it is made from soybean extract, flour, mushrooms, salt, and water. It may be used as a substitute for black soy sauce. The Pearl River Bridge brand from China is good. It is sold in Chinese grocery stores, especially those that carry goods from mainland China.

Storing: Store as black soy sauce.

Thin Soy Sauce

Thin soy sauce, also known as light soy sauce, is made from soybeans, flour, salt, and water. It is topaz-colored, but thinner and saltier than black soy sauce. Use only the varieties imported from China, Hong Kong, and Taiwan. I prefer the kind made by Koon Chun Company of Hong Kong.

Sugar (Rock)

Rock sugar comes in large crystals. It is light amber in color and is not as sweet as granulated sugar, for it releases sweetness slowly.

Spring Roll Skins
(See page 10)

Tangerine Peel (Dried)

This is also known as old tangerine peel or mandarin orange peel. It is coffee-colored, has a condensed sweet fragrance, and is used to flavor food.

Storing: Keep indefinitely in a tightly covered jar. The longer it is kept, the better it is.

Taro
(See page 30)

Turnip (Chinese White)

This vegetable is shaped like a big sweet potato, with a white body and translucent skin. Choose one that is firm and heavy. They are sold in Oriental food stores.

Storing: Refrigerated, it will keep about a week.

Vinegar (Chenkong)

Chenkong (also romanized as Chen-Chiang) is a large city in Kiangsu Province of China. This vinegar is dark brown, tangy, and spicy. With more strength than Chinese red vinegar, it is sold in Chinese grocery stores.

Vinegar (Chinese Red)

In the bottle, this rice vinegar is clear. But it turns red within hours after the bottle is opened. Used in cooking as well as dips, it is sold in Chinese grocery stores.

Storing: Will keep for months if it is tightly covered.

Water Chestnut Powder

Used in making pastries or as batter to coat deep-fried foods for crispness, this lumpy, grayish flour made from water chestnuts must be sifted before using. It is sold in Chinese grocery stores.

Storing: Store as flour.

Water Chestnuts

The fresh variety are quarter-sized buttonlike bulbs, with deep purple skins. They grow in shallow, muddy water. When fresh and young, the meat is crystal white, sweet, juicy, and crisp. If old, they become starchy and less sweet. They must be skinned; then they can be eaten fresh as fruit, or as a cooked vegetable with meat and poultry, glazed in sugar, or ground into powder to make sweet pastry.

Canned water chestnuts are peeled and canned in water; they are still crisp, but have lost their sweetness. Use them as a vegetable cooked with meat and poultry.

Storing: Let the mud stay on the skin to protect fresh water chestnuts from drying out; refrigerated they will keep for 4 to 5 days. Or you may wash and peel them, put them in a jar, cover with cold water, refrigerate, and change water every other day. Canned water chestnuts, stored in water in the same manner, will keep for weeks. Freezing is not desirable; the meat becomes spongy.

Wheat Starch

Wheat starch—wheat flour with the gluten removed—is used to make very light, delicate translucent skins for some dainty pastries such as hah gau (see page 62). Without the gluten, the dough made from wheat starch lacks elasticity and is therefore more fragile to handle. Wheat starch is sold in Chinese grocery stores.

Storing: Store as flour.

Wonton Skins
(See page 13)

Wine (Chinese Shaohsing Wine and Pale Dry Sherry)

A small amount of wine is used in many dishes not just for the flavor but also to eliminate the odor in seafood, poultry, and meat. Shaohsing wine is a rice wine widely used by the Chinese in cooking. We also drink it warm with the meal. If Shaohsing wine is not available, pale dry sherry is the best substitute.

Yu Choy

Yu Choy is one of the most delicious Chinese green vegetables. It has tiny yellow flowers, green leaves, and stems which are all to be eaten. It has more flavor than bok choy and is also crisper. You can buy it in bundles in Chinese grocery stores.

Storing: Keep in refrigerator; use within 4 days.

SHOPPING LIST

Authentic Chinese cooking requires using the right ingredients; shopping well is almost as important as cooking well. I have provided a list of ingredients in both Chinese and English since the English labeling of products by Chinese canning companies is not always reliable. For example, a bottle may be labeled "Soy Sauce" and in Chinese "Thin Soy Sauce."

   With this list you can point to what you want in English and the Chinese clerk will be able to read the precise Chinese equivalent. This applies also to fresh vegetables, where the language problem can be especially confusing, since some Chinese vegetables may not have an English-language equivalent.

ABALONE (CANNED) 罐頭鮑魚

AGAR-AGAR (TAI CHOY) 東洋大菜

ANISE (STAR) 八　　角

BAMBOO LEAVES (DRIED) 種　　葉

BAMBOO SHOOTS (CANNED) 罐頭竹筍

BEAN CURD (FIVE-FRAGRANCE) 五香豆腐

BEAN CURD (FRESH) 豆　　腐

BEAN CURD SKINS 軟豆腐皮

BEAN CURD CHEESE (RED) 紅南乳

BEAN CURD PUFFS (FRIED) 炸 豆 腐 泡

BEAN PASTE (SWEET RED) 罐 頭 紅 豆 沙

BEAN SPROUTS (FRESH) 綠 豆 芽

BEAN SAUCE (GROUND) 磨 原 豉

BEAN SAUCE (SZECHWAN SWEET) 四 川 甜 麵 醬

BEAN SAUCE (SZECHWAN HOT) 四 川 辣 豆 辦 醬

BLACK BEANS (SALTED) 豆 豉

BOK CHOY (FRESH) 白 菜

CHINESE CELERY CABBAGE (TIENTSIN CABBAGE) 天 津 白 菜

CABBAGE (SNOW) 雪 裡 紅 (罐頭)

CHILI PEPPERS (DRIED) 乾 辣 椒

CHILI SAUCE (CHINESE) 辣 椒 醬

CLOUD EARS 雲 耳

COCONUT MILK (UNSWEETENED) 香 菜

CORIANDER (FRESH) 椰 汁 (不甜的)

CURRY PASTE 咖 哩 醬

FIVE-FRAGRANCE POWDER 五 香 粉

FLOWER PEPPERCORNS 花 椒

GINGER ROOT (FRESH) 薑

HAM (CHINESE AND SMITHFIELD) 火 腿

HOISIN SAUCE 海鮮醬

JELLYFISH SKIN 海蜇皮

LEMON SAUCE 檸檬醬

LILY BUDS (DRIED) 金 針

LOTUS LEAVES (DRIED) 蓮 葉

MUSHROOMS (CHINESE DRIED) 冬菇

MUSHROOMS (GOLDEN, CANNED) 金菇 (罐頭)

MUSHROOMS (STRAW, CANNED) 草菇 (罐頭)

MUSTARD GREENS (PICKLED) 咸酸菜

MUSTARD PICKLE (SZECHWAN) 四川炸菜

NOODLES, FRESH EGG 新鮮蛋麵

NOODLES (BEAN THREAD) 粉 絲

RICE NOODLES (DRIED) 乾米粉

NOODLES (SAH HO RICE NOODLES) 新鮮沙河粉

OIL (CHILI) 辣椒油

OIL (SESAME) 蔴 油

OYSTER SAUCE 蠔油

PLUM SAUCE 蘇梅醬

RICE (GLUTINOUS) 糯米

RICE POWDER 粘米粉

RICE POWDER (GLUTINOUS) 糯米粉

SAH GOH 沙葛

SATÉ SAUCE 沙爹醬

SAUSAGES (CHINESE DUCK LIVER) 鴨肝腸

SAUSAGE (CHINESE PORK) 臘腸

SHRIMP (DRIED) 蝦米

SHRIMP CHIPS 蝦片

SHAO MAI SKINS 燒賣皮

SNOW PEAS (FRESH) 雪豆

SOY SAUCE (BLACK) 醬油 (陶大)

SOY SAUCE (DOUBLE BLACK) 双老抽

SOY SAUCE (FISH-FLAVORED) 魚露

SOY SAUCE (MUSHROOM) 草菇老抽

SOY SAUCE (THIN) 生　抽

SUGAR (ROCK) 冰　糖

SPRING ROLL SKINS 春卷皮

TANGERINE PEEL (DRIED) 陳　皮

TARO (FRESH) 荔甫芋頭

TURNIP (CHINESE WHITE) 大蘿蔔

VINEGAR (CHENKONG) 鎮江醋

VINEGAR (CHINESE RED) 大紅浙醋

WATER CHESTNUT POWDER 馬蹄粉

WATER CHESTNUTS 馬　蹄

WHEAT STARCH 澄麵粉

WONTON SKINS 雲吞皮

WINE (SHAOHSING) 紹興酒

YU CHOY 油　菜

TABLE OF METRIC EQUIVALENTS

Weight (common units)

1 ounce	28.35 grams
1 pound	453.59 grams
1 gram	0.035 ounces
1 kilogram	2.21 pounds

Volume (common units)

1 cup	16 tablespoons
	8 fluid ounces
	236.6 milliliters
1 tablespoon	3 teaspoons
	0.5 fluid ounce
	14.8 milliliters
1 teaspoon	4.9 milliliters
1 liter	1,000 milliliters
	1.06 quarts
1 bushel	4 pecks
1 peck	8 quarts
1 gallon	4 quarts
1 quart	2 pints
1 pint	2 cups
	473.2 milliliters

INDEX

223